The POWER
of the Professoriate

Demands, Challenges, and Opportunities in 21st Century Higher Education

By Nicholas D. Young and Lynne M. Celli

Atwood Publishing
Madison WI

The Power of the Professoriate: Demands, Challenges, and Opportunities in 21st Century Higher Education
By Nicholas D. Young and Lynne M. Celli
© Atwood Publishing 2017
www.atwoodpublishing.com

Cover design by Six-O-Six Design

Library of Congress Cataloging-in-Publication Data

Names: Young, Nicholas D., 1967- author. | Celli, Lynne M., author.
Title: The power of the professoriate : demands, challenges and opportunities
   in 21st century higher education / by Nicholas D. Young, PhD, EdD and
   Lynne M. Celli, PhD.
Description: Madison, WI : Atwood Publishing, [2017]
Identifiers: LCCN 2017036059 | ISBN 9780997248944 (softcover : alk. paper)
Subjects: LCSH: College teachers—Professional relationships.
Classification: LCC LB1778 .Y69 2017 | DDC 378.1/25—dc23 LC record available at https://lccn.loc.gov

Acknowledgments

Nicholas D. Young

Lynne and I are indebted to our colleagues who worked diligently on their individual chapters of this book. Your expertise and deep commitment to higher education in general, and the role of the professor in particular, made this project personally and professionally meaningful to us. Please know that your contributions are both recognized and appreciated. I also wish to acknowledge Sue Clark and Samantha Grace Dias for their respective editorial contributions to this book. Both were part of our "dream team" and were instrumental in making this book a reality. Sue was incredibly gracious in devoting her time and expertise to this project. Please know that we are grateful and appreciative of your efforts. Samantha, who has worked with us now through countless books, has also become an extended member of our family. Thank you, Sam, for continuing to sign up for these projects. Your support makes more of a difference than you realize.

On a personal note, I want to use this forum to thank a dear aunt of mine, Barbara Young, for being such a positive influence throughout my life. Aunt Barbara ("Aunt Bobbie" to the members of the large Young clan who call Acworth, New Hampshire, the home base for their "tribe") is one of those special people who thinks of others before herself. Although she did not have children of her own, she has long assumed a mother figure status with so many members of the Young family, including my 76-year-old father, David. (Their generation started with a dozen siblings, and many have done their part to keep the family name strong for the foreseeable future; thus achieving any kind of status with them is no small feat!) While I am merely one of many who think fondly of Aunt Bobbie, I want her to know that I hold her in the highest regard and I promise not to tell anyone how much I appreciated her allowing me to sip a little wine from time to time when I was underage. Aunt Bobbie, please know that your "tribe" loves you very much.

Lynne M. Celli

For my part of this professional effort, I would like to thank all our contributing authors. Without your expertise and wisdom, this publication would not be possible. You should each feel immensely proud of your respective endeavors to improve the field of education.

I would also like to offer a special acknowledgment of my father, Angelo Celli, who passed away on May 27, 2015, after a valiant battle with cancer. You, Dad, were "the wind beneath my wings." You always encouraged me and told me "ever to excel." Thank you for the inspiration to be the best I could be and to continue your legacy of excellence. You will forever be missed.

Table of Contents

Current Trends in the Professoriate 7
by Nicholas D. Young and Lynne M. Celli

CHAPTER 1: Navigating the Professoriate: Hiring, Evaluation,
and Promotion 15
by Nicholas D. Young and Elizabeth Jean

CHAPTER 2: Connections in the Classroom:
The Faculty Member's Role in Relational Retention 27
by Christine N. Michael

CHAPTER 3: At the Heart of the College Experience:
Transforming Groups Into Meaningful Teams by
Harnessing the Power of Affiliation-Based Teaching
Practices 49
by Janice A. Fedor and Nicholas D. Young

CHAPTER 4: The Professor's Role in Teaching Subject-
Specific Scholarly Writing 61
by Nadine Bonda

CHAPTER 5: Leadership in the Professoriate:
Components Necessary for Growth 75
by Lynne M. Celli

CHAPTER 6: Student Recruitment and Retention:
Essential Faculty Contributions 87
by Judith L. Klimkiewicz

CHAPTER 7: Professors as Catalysts:
Connecting College with Community 103
by Linda Denault

CHAPTER 8: Academic Identity:
 The Changing Landscape of the Professoriate 117
 by Rick Roque

CHAPTER 9: The Fundamentals of Virtual Teaching:
 Opportunities and Approaches 127
 by Nicholas D. Young and Elizabeth Jean

Index 143

About the Primary Authors 151

About the Chapter Authors 153

Current Trends in the Professoriate

By Nicholas D. Young and Lynne M. Celli

The role of the professoriate is changing quite profoundly, in ways few could have imagined only a decade ago, yet based on the shifting demographics and demands of current and future students (Szybinski and Jordan 2010), perhaps these changes are not occurring as quickly as is needed. While faculty of yesteryear focused on teaching and were assured security through tenure, today's professors find themselves in a multifaceted role and without guarantee of a tenure-track position. This slippery slope has caused angst among adjunct, full-time, and tenure-track professors and postsecondary institutions alike who must now find innovative ways to reach and teach the modern student. While the job security of contemporary professorship positions continues to evolve, Hainline, Gaines, Long Feather, Padilla, and Terry (2010) underscore that tried-and-true approaches to classroom instruction have concurrently become obsolete. Consequently, contemporary professors are now tasked with transforming academia into an interactive learning environment that honors scholarly explorations, real-world experiences, and self-exploration opportunities— all bundled together for less than a bargain-basement price.

In several areas, the twenty-first century evolution of the professoriate is immense. Scholars entering higher education must now know that the role of faculty at universities and colleges is multifaceted; thus, before entering into academia, the expectations, responsibilities, and accountability for prospective candidates need to be firmly understood. Some of the most glaring shifts in the profession have come in the degree of institutional commitment as well as the level of expectation placed on faculty of all classifications.

Tenure-Track vs. Non-tenure-Track (Part-Time and Contingent) Faculty

The current population of America's professors are aging at a dramatic pace (Hainline et al. 2010). As these faculty retire, they are regularly replaced by contingent faculty or, as some call them, non-tenure-track, part-time faculty. This trend began decades ago. In 1993, the American Association of University Professors stated that part-time faculty made up 38% of the entire professional pool. In comparison, more than 68% of the total instructor ranks at some contemporary higher education institutions are now designated as part-time, non-tenure-track, or contingent (Bonetta 2011; Kezar 2012). This alarming statistic reveals the evolving demographics of the professoriate, and some contend that this decline in tenure-track positions compromises the very essence of the quality of higher education (Hackmann and McCarthy 2013). Under this argument, an increasingly smaller percentage of professors are now devoted solely to teaching, scholarship, and service as more and more of them are forced to accept part-time wages that almost always necessitate employment at one or more additional higher education institutions simultaneously or between a college or university and another private or public entity (Coalition on the Academic Workforce 2012; Concordia University 2015).

Professors who are forced to have mixed employment loyalties are more likely to be stretched thin and have insufficient time to meet the full demands that accompany the contemporary concurrent rigors of teaching, scholarship, and service. Often, service to the home university suffers first. Most, if not all, professors would agree that time challenges can serve as a substantial obstacle to an active program of scholarship as well as to ongoing professional development endeavors. Admittedly, just as there are exceptions to every rule, there are part-time and contingent faculty who have discovered the secret to striking the proper balance between sufficient employment, teaching responsibilities, and scholarship. Some are even able to make an institutional contribution in the area of service as well. However, one need only witness the challenges that tenured and other full-time faculty experience in meeting the broad expectations of their role to have an appreciation of how especially challenging this task becomes for those who have an economic disadvantage requiring additional employment.

Changing Expectations of the Professoriate

Over the past three decades, the degree of employment or, said another way, the level of institutional commitment to their faculty has moved in the direction of an increasing number of part-time and adjunct faculty on college campuses; all the while, the expectations placed on those who have remained at any given institution of higher education have likely increased considerably. Many institutions now commonly cast full-time faculty into leadership roles, such as program directors, while increasing employment expectations in the areas of student retention, recruitment, and public outreach. On top of this, colleges and universities also expect their professors to adapt to changing instructional methods, including staying current with new technologies, while remaining active as scholars and contributors to the larger body of research and knowledge. High expectations are certainly not limited to full-time and tenure-track faculty; more and more higher education institutions are taking advantage of the growing talent pool of part-time and contingent faculty who have been unable to land a coveted permanent position yet have remained loyal to their assigned department or program. Increasingly, contingent faculty are asked to contribute to institutional and program development activities while also demonstrating continued subject-matter currency through ongoing scholarship or other forms of professional development.

Essentially all colleges and universities have been compelled to change for numerous reasons, not the least of which is to become more responsive to the fiscal concerns of their constituencies. While recognizing these realities and the many pressures faced by higher education administrators, we purposely wanted to focus this book on the trends, expectations, challenges, and potential approaches that may be of interest or of some benefit to all those who are striving to advance the professoriate in particular. We are intentionally not segmenting professors into the traditional faculty classifications (i.e., tenured, full-time, part-time, or adjunct), except when to do so is of some informational value to describe trends. We understand that profound changes have occurred in our ranks, and we wish to acknowledge the important role and responsibilities of all who assume critically significant higher education teaching duties.

Our motivation for writing this book is rooted in several convictions:

- Our belief that the professoriate is a unique and changing landscape—one that merits special attention because it is distinctly different both from any other teaching capacity and from its historical past

- Our concern regarding the nature of the professorship, tenure and non-tenure positions alike, with all the new roles and expectations that have become superimposed upon them
- Our knowledge that the professor plays an increasingly important role in student retention and college recruitment
- Our desire to identify and share best teaching practices and new ideas regarding the changing world of the college/university professor
- Our interest in sharing our combined years of experience in higher education fulfilling the major tenets of the role, including teaching, scholarship, and service
- Our passion in helping the next generation of professors explore and find career and life success in academia, understanding that this cannot be completed in isolation because it requires a team dedicated to the success of students

We chose the first part of the title, *The Power of the Professoriate,* to underscore the importance of the role of professors and the way in which they influence the educational journey of postsecondary students. It is not enough to simply teach; the expectations of the modern professor far exceed those of past decades and are perhaps more extensive and complex than ever before.

Written by a decidedly seasoned team of professors and scholars, this book seeks to understand past professorial practice and, with a keen eye toward the future, aims to uncover and explain the twenty-first century roles and expectations of the new professor, shedding light on the intricacies that few are aware of until they are confronted with the realities of the position. Written in similar format to other practitioner-based texts, each chapter of this book offers a look at relevant literature, discusses its implications specifically for the professor, and includes a helpful "Points to Remember" section.

It is our sincere hope that professors, both seasoned and new, will find this book to be a valuable resource and guide, offering a wide range of topics to enhance their practice. Contact information for each chapter author also has been provided so that readers can reach out to them to obtain more information; engage in conversation; and share their experiences, struggles, and successes as a fellow professor or as one who wishes to enter the world of the professoriate.

About the Book

Although a considerable amount has been written about the professoriate, questions still remain. For this reason, *The Power of the Professoriate: Demands, Challenges and Opportunities in 21st Century Higher Education* covers the following topics in depth: what the modern professoriate looks like; thoughts on tackling scholarly writing in the classroom; effective teaching practices to consider, including teams and relational groups; professorial components necessary for growth; college and community relations; and the world of virtual education and online teaching. The chapters are organized to start at the beginning of a career in academia and lead the reader through to the burgeoning world of online learning. The following overview provides the reader with a preview of the various concepts included in this book.

Chapter 1 was written by Nicholas D. Young and Elizabeth Jean to provide an understanding of the hiring, evaluation, and promotion procedures and practices available to professors. Here, the authors explain how the job of the professor has changed over time to include not just teaching but also scholarship and service and how those requirements are viewed and judged by postsecondary institutions. In addition, the nuances between adjunct, non-tenured, and tenured full-time professorships are explored to include the expectations by classification type. Some consideration of commonly understood must-haves in the tenure-seeking professor's dossier are identified as well.

In Chapter 2, Christine N. Michael discusses the role of faculty in the quest for relational retention of college students. The statistics for low-income, first-generation students are staggering: these students are four times more likely to complete only one year of college prior to dropping out, and more than 40% leave after six years without a degree (Engle and Tinto 2008). It is no wonder, the author argues, that building relations between student and professor becomes a priority, as the professor may be able to use positive persuasion and relationship building to help students persevere through the unknown college experience. Using case studies to prove her point, the author leaves no doubt that faculty are key to relational retention.

Appreciating that students come to college with different needs, agendas, abilities, and learning styles, Chapter 3, written by Janice A. Fedor and Nicholas D. Young, focuses on Affiliation-Based Teaching (ABT). Using a framework that values work experience and individual learning styles, the professor is tasked with motivating students both intrinsically and extrinsically through small groups where students have had similar experiences, learning strengths, or learning weaknesses. Understanding that there is a time investment involved before reaping the benefits of such teaching and learning, the authors suggest that ABT is most useful for courses in which student interaction and active engagement are paramount.

In Chapter 4, Nadine Bonda explores the role of the professor in teaching subject-specific scholarly writing, which differs significantly from basic writing skills. Scholarly writing uses reason to make an argument, is written for an informed reader, and is grounded in scholarly literature (Bair and Mader 2013). The author explains the stages of learning necessary to write in academic fashion, being sure to remind the reader of the need to think critically and analytically about the subject matter as well as the importance of professor feedback as a tool for improvement. Because scholarly writing is entirely different from everyday writing, it can be anxiety-producing to the student; thus, it is the job of the professor to describe the necessary writing conventions used for the discipline at hand, all of which is explained in this chapter.

Because leadership has become an intricate part of the professoriate on many college campuses, it is important to define and understand the components necessary to promote and expand that role. Written by Lynne M. Celli, Chapter 5 offers a critical look at expanding the leadership role of the professor through supportive professional development, a review and modification of processes and procedures related to hiring and promotion, as well as emphasizing quality teaching. The author goes on to further describe these components, and she concludes by emphasizing the importance of creating effective leaders and teams at postsecondary institutions by thinking strategically.

In Chapter 6, Judith L. Klimkiewicz examines the significance of faculty in student recruitment and retention. Today's educational climate, replete with declining college enrollments, makes critical the need to bridge the gap between student enrollment and graduation rates. Professors fill that gap through almost daily contact with students whether it is in class, during office hours, mentoring, or in social settings. The author describes the role of the professor, strategies that promote student retention, and conditions that increase retention. Through this chapter, the reader will gain an increased appreciation for the role that faculty play in the successful recruitment and retention of college students at all degree levels.

Connecting the college with the community to promote meaningful, real-world experiences is the focus of Chapter 7. Written by Linda E. Denault, this chapter examines the professor as a catalyst by which students advance their education and increase their future success through authentic work in the community. Looking first at the historical perspective and then at the contemporary perspective, the reader is able to see the advancements and connections that can be made through experiential learning opportunities in promoting twenty-first century skills. Using the professor as a facilitator to such work is central to addressing issues of relevance and rigor. The author then discusses the impact on the brain, professorial outreach, the role of technology, and potential drawbacks to community connections. The chapter concludes with a reminder that the professor who seeks relevancy between curricula and community connections will ultimately benefit his or her students in ways that far exceed those of the traditional classroom.

In Chapter 8, Rick Roque describes the factors currently forcing change in higher education—which include technology, student demographics, and economic conditions—as well as the impact these factors have on coursework content, structure, and delivery methods. The author explains that because of these factors, higher education has been forced to revisit its mission and faculty preparation to more adequately address the needs of current students. Through this chapter, readers learn about the changing culture of the professoriate as well as the keys to success in this evolving college climate. In the end, the author reminds readers that the rapid pace of change requires postsecondary institutions to re-examine, adjust, adapt, and implement a plethora of practices to meet the new demands of the contemporary higher education consumer.

Last, but not least, Chapter 9 looks at the fundamentals of virtual education with an eye on the trends and opportunities available to both professors and their students. Nicholas D. Young and Elizabeth Jean ask readers to recall a time when brick-and-mortar classroom teaching was the norm, lectures were commonplace, and assignments were completed with pen and paper. Fast-forward to today's exciting world of online learning incorporating various sources—from Massive Open Online Courses and

Open Educational Resources to TED Talks and Khan Academy, to name just a few. Professors are now tasked with making lessons three dimensional, interactive, and potentially tailored to individual learning styles. The authors look at who virtual learners are, what delivery models and instructional tools are available to professors, and how social media is influencing traditional learning. In the end, a discussion of the principles of online teaching shows readers what professors need to know to be successful in the up-and-coming virtual world

References

American Association of University Professors. 1993. *The status of non-tenure-track faculty* Washington, DC: Author. Retrieved from https://www.aaup.org/report/status-non-tenure-track-faculty

Bair, M. A., and C. E. Mader. 2013. Academic writing at the graduate level: Improving the curriculum through faculty collaboration. *Journal of University Teaching and Learning Practice*, 10(1). Retrieved from http://ro.uow.edu.au/jutlp/vol10/iss1/4/

Bonetta, L. 2011, February 11. Moving up the academic ladder. *Science.* Retrieved from www.sciencemag.org/careers/features/2011/02/moving_academic_ladder

Coalition on the Academic Workforce. 2012, June. *A portrait of part-time faculty members: A summary of findings on part-time faculty respondents to the Coalition on the Academic Workforce survey of contingent faculty members and instructors.* Retrieved from http://www.academic workforce.org/CAW_portrait_2012.pdf

Concordia University. 2015. *How to become an adjunct professor: Job, education, salary.* Retrieved from http://education.cu-portland.edu/blog/teaching-careers/adjunct-professor/#duties

Engle, J., and V. Tinto. 2008. Moving beyond access: College success for low-income, first-generation students. Washington, DC: Pell Institute for the Study of Opportunity in Education.

Hackmann, D. G., and M.M. McCarthy. 2013. What constitutes a critical mass? An investigation of faculty staffing patterns in educational leadership programs. *Journal of Research on Leadership Education* 8(1): 5–27.

Hainline, L., M. Gaines, C. Long Feather, E. Padilla, and E. Terry. 2010. Changing students, faculty, and institutions in the twenty-first century. *Peer Review: The Future of Faculty: Collaborating to Cultivate Change* 12(3).

Kezar, A. 2012, November/December. Spanning the great divide between tenure-track and non-tenure-track faculty. *Change: The Magazine of Higher Learning* 44(6). Retrieved from http://www.changemag.org/Archives/Back%20Issues/2012/November-December%202012/spanning-great-divide-full.html

Szybinski, D., and T. Jordan. 2010. Navigating the future of the professoriate. *The Future of Faculty: Collaborating to Cultivate Change* 12(3). Retrieved from https://www.aacu.org/publications-research/periodicals/navigating-future-Professoriate

CHAPTER 1

Navigating the Professoriate

Hiring, Evaluation, and Promotion

By Nicholas D. Young and Elizabeth Jean

While teaching and mentoring students has traditionally been the first job among many for professors, learning to navigate the world of the professorship provides a learning curve all its own. The professoriate is all encompassing with continued high expectations in teaching, service, and scholarship (Albertine 2013). This triad becomes the basis on which college and university professors are judged (Curry 2006). From hiring to evaluation to promotion, each step of the professorship follows certain guidelines that are almost exactly the same regardless of the institution, but they are often unknown to the professor until he or she is knee deep in the world of postsecondary education (Bonetta 2011).

Hiring

The road to academic professorship must be carefully crafted; it is simply not enough to have been a teacher or superintendent, an esteemed business person or an entrepreneur, a scientist or artist (Roney and Ulerick 2013). Most institutions will hire adjuncts first. This approach is a cost-saving measure, an opportunity to evaluate up-and-coming professors, and a way to ensure the competitive nature of the tenure track. Another track in academia is a nontenured faculty position, which holds no advancement timeline or guaranteed job but often offers professors the same titles (Bonetta 2011).

Depending on the university or college, each leg of the professorial journey when pursuing a tenure-track position takes approximately seven years to complete. A traditional academic trajectory would include time spent as an adjunct professor, assistant professor, associate professor, and finally a fully tenured professor. An adjunct professor will frequently need to teach a large course load—possibly at several institutions—for little in return. For example, an adjunct professor may teach five classes, work 20–30 hours a week, and only make $15,000 a year (Hall 2015). Although this short-term work is incredibly taxing, the long-term gain is often worth the initial effort exerted.

Both full- and part-time, non-tenure-track positions have shown growth in the United States. In 2007, just shy of 20% of all appointments were non-tenure-track as compared to 13% in 1975, while tenure-track appointments fell to just 9.9% as compared to 20.3% during that same time period (Bonetta 2011). More recent data shows that "two-thirds of full- and part-time faculty members nationwide are off the tenure track" (Kezar 2012). Hackmann and McCarthy explain that there is considerable controversy regarding part-time instructors; they are usually current practitioners in the field of study, but some believe that adjuncts "diminish program quality" (2013, 6).

Non-tenure-track positions generally have higher workloads, renewable contracts, and no guarantee of specific salaries like their tenured counterparts; however, there is no pressure to complete a promotion package every seven years to advance. Adjuncts sometimes find inequities at the institutions they work for, including a lack of benefits, lower pay, different working conditions, and little or no time to devote to campus involvement (Coalition on the Academic Workforce 2012; Concordia University 2015). Nevertheless, the path to advancement is virtually the same regardless of tenure or non-tenure; a professor simply chooses stability and security for less pressure. For professors whose end goal is full tenure, the professor (at any level) must continuously work hard not only at teaching but also in the areas of scholarship and service.

Evaluation and Promotion

Greater demands at the university level by accrediting boards have trickled down to influence and shape the promotion and evaluation systems in place for professors who wish to move through the hierarchy of professorship titles. To ensure a professional atmosphere with rigorous standards, colleges and universities have increased the demands on professors and tightened up promotion and tenure requirements. Within each seven-year cycle are yearly evaluations and reviews based on predetermined goals as well as tasks to show growth in the three areas of professorship: teaching, scholarship, and service (Plater 2008).

Evaluation

Teaching is a fundamental task for any professor, and it is the first of three parts to process for evaluation and promotion at most institutions (American International College [AIC] 2016; Curry 2006; Dakota State University [DSU] 2016; Middlebury College 2016; University of Washington Dean's Office, College of Arts and Science 2012). While this may seem the easiest part of the professoriate, modern-day professors are expected to not only show up and lecture in front of students but also make valuable contributions to student learning, growth, and development. Furthermore, a plethora of colleges and universities are currently adopting higher standards for their professors, making the art of teaching even more rigorous and demanding (AIC 2016; DSU 2016; Middlebury College 2016; University of Washington 2012).

Essentially, professors are expected to become experts in their disciplines. They must develop and evaluate courses, which means that they need to be able to convey the skills and knowledge inherent in any content area as well as use instructional technology to enhance their courses. Dakota State University (2016, 6) expresses various aspects of course creation and evaluation as "critical to professional achievement," and within DSU's teaching section, professors are expected to prove themselves as having each of the following:

- Content Expertise: knowledge, skills, and abilities
- Instructional Design: designing, sequencing, and presenting content as well as student evaluation and assessment
- Instructional delivery: interactive skills
- Course management: organizing, managing, and operating a course
- Instructional technology: appropriate use of technology by staff and students
- Advising: consulting with students, providing guidance, planning, goal setting

DSU (2016) advises professors that there are two categories of teaching performance: basic or high performance. High-performing professors would show "significant" skills described as "exceptional in terms of scope, prestige of venue, impact on the audience/profession, importance to the university, etc., rather than on routine elements" (DSU 2016, 9). These categories are further divided into "meets expectations" and "exceeds expectations" to identify the best professors and hopefully spur on the marginal ones.

At American International College (AIC) in Springfield, Massachusetts, the task of teaching is described as "effectiveness in teaching" (2016, 1), and the college takes a more reflective angle in its teaching evaluations by asking professors to examine the following areas:

- *Student evaluations:* summarize evaluations received from students
- *Data:* courses taught with enrollment
- *New approaches:* curriculum or innovative approaches introduced into the teaching
- *Integration:* personal scholarly work woven into the classes taught
- *Advising:* assessment of advising role
- *Classroom observation report:* written reports from peers, chair, director, or dean
- *Goals:* personal goals set and progress toward meeting those goals

AIC then breaks down the category into five levels: (1) does not meet expectations, (2) approaching expectations, (3) consistently meets all expectations, (4) performance beyond normal expectations, and (5) distinguished. These levels are used as a tool to evaluate and promote professors. The University of Washington (2016) has similar categories and levels, and Middlebury College (2016, n.p.) goes so far as to indicate that it "expect[s] to appoint to the faculty men and women of exceptional promise and achievement as teachers and as scholars."

All colleges and universities fall within this spectrum of teaching expectations for their professors, regardless of whether these professors are on tenure- or non-tenure-tracks. Many institutions include advising within the realm of teaching, but many others, including DSU (2016) and Oregon State University (OSU 2015) separate it out, giving it equal consideration when evaluating a professor's ability to be of value to the school. Several institutions (AIC 2016; Middlebury College 2016; University of Washington 2012) clearly value scholarship by asking instructors how they have integrated scholarly work into course activities, increasing student engagement, and authentic research experience.

Scholarship. The second of the three evaluation tools and perhaps the most difficult to achieve, scholarship generally means that the professor has made written contributions to existing literature and research in some way enhancing and expanding what is known about a particular body of knowledge. It may include research that leads to publications, such as edited book chapters, peer-reviewed journal articles, or conference proceedings. It may also mean that the professor has engaged in specific research or grant work that may or may not be associated with the college or university. At some institutions, such as DSU (2016, 13), scholarship is reserved for "faculty holding professorial rank," while it is difficult to tell what, if any, distinction is made at AIC (2016).

What is clear, however, is that both institutions value scholarship and view it as inherent to the job of the professor. DSU describes scholarly activities as (1) the "development of knowledge within the professional community … with productivity in the areas of publication, presentation, exhibition, and/or performance" and (2) the "development of professional skills and standing within the professional community … [via] recognition by peers and others for expertise in the academic discipline" (2016, 14). As with teaching, DSU also divides scholarship into basic and high-performance categories and then further subdivides it into "meets expectations" and "exceeds expectations." These classifications offer a clearly defined model that reveals institutional expectation of scholarship for professors.

Other institutions (AIC 2016; Middlebury College 2016) express the need for scholarship in a more reflective manner by asking the professor to describe the contributions made, including basic documentation of accomplishments, commentary on whether goals were set and met, and explanations of why and how a professor might rectify any unmet goals in the following year. The professor is specifically asked to show his or her "effectiveness as a scholar" (AIC 2016, 2). Some colleges and universities divide scholarship into levels of proficiency. A highly proficient professor would complete grant work as well as make extensive progress in writing and publishing in peer-reviewed journals, publish conference papers, and academic books. A less proficient professor might not have a specific plan for scholarly work, would attend few conferences and might not present, would rarely participate in campus-offered professional development, and would not be current in his or her own field. Administrators at Middlebury College (2016, n.p.) contend that "a faculty engaged in scholarship enriches the intellectual climate" and that such work "is a prerequisite for promotion to tenure" when it is of high quality and recognized by others outside the institution.

These institutions, like all other colleges and universities, are looking for high-quality scholarship, but they go about it in different ways (OSU 2015; University of Washington Rules Coordination Office 2016). Even at a Turkish university, where professors are scored yearly on a 1–100 scale, 50 or more points must come from scholarship (Uzuner-Smith and Englander 2015). It is clear from these examples that postsecondary institutions place a premium on scholarship; however, service to the college or university and the community is also expected by each professor being evaluated.

Service. The final piece to the promotion package is that of service, or being of service to others at the institution or in the larger community. This service might be in the form of departmental committees, ethics boards, or internal peer-reviewed journal boards. It is a "donation of time, effort and energy, without significant compensation, to activities that draw upon the faculty member's professional expertise and knowledge" (DSU 2016, 18). Once again, colleges and universities demonstrate a broad spectrum of how this evaluation component may be handled by the individual professor.

DSU (2016) requires professors to submit documentation in three areas of service: (1) university—participation in academic and university functions, activities, and committees; (2) discipline or profession—participation in professional organizations; and (3) community—participation in activities that benefit K–12 schools, agencies, corporations, and organizations other than the university. In contrast, AIC asks for descriptions of service, identification of "special assignments," and leadership roles held (2016, 2). AIC also requests "commentary" on goals set and met (or not met and why) as well as descriptions and evidence of "other work contributing to ... effectiveness in service and institutional participation" (2016, 2).

At Middlebury College (2016, n.p.), service is any activity that benefits the institution, such as "departmental, program, and committee responsibilities, activities with student organizations, participation in admissions or alumni activities" and the like. The evaluation materials there are less specific about the way in which professors go about the process and how they integrate themselves into the activity. The University of Washington Rules Coordination Office (2016, n.p.) even includes organizational work as well as recruitment and retention of students as service work, stating that both categories "make an important contribution and should be included in the individual faculty profile." As with teaching and scholarship, many institutions further divide the service category to help professors better understand and work toward the highest levels of professional conduct and service to both the institution and the community.

The three-legged stool of teaching, scholarship, and service is highly valued and the basis for all upward movement within the ranks of the professorship. It is not enough to excel only at teaching; the professor seeking a positive review and/or a full-tenured position must also show a continued history of teaching, scholarship, and service within the college or university community. DSU (2016, 18) adds this caveat to its evaluation and promotion package: "Professorial faculty over a six-year period (prior to tenure) must show some involvement in all three areas—not in every annual review, but over the course of time." It is this notion of sustained excellence in teaching, scholarship, and service over time that provides the basis for promotion from assistant to associate to full-tenured professor.

Promotion

Yearly evaluations aside, moving from adjunct to full-tenured professor takes considerable planning, time, and effort on the part of the professor and good judgment on the part of the institution. The promotion packet is lengthy, the process arduous, and professors are not automatically granted a tenured position when they become an associate professor; tenure is a separate decision often made using subjective judgments (Saltzman 2008).

Promotion process. Most colleges and universities employ similar standards for the evaluation and promotion processes when examining non-tenure-track and tenure-track professors—the difference being that the professor wishing to advance must show a six-year history of exemplary teaching, scholarship, and service to be considered for advanced professorial positions. Depending on the institution, one of the three categories may be emphasized over the others. For example, a research university may value scholarship over teaching and service, while a teaching college may place more significance on teaching over scholarship and service (Saltzman 2008).

In general terms, when a professor submits his or her packet for consideration, the dean and/or committee will evaluate the packet, taking into account the job evaluations completed thus far, along with all self-study documentation submitted. In the case of AIC (2016, 5), the dean assigns a rating to each of the three categories (i.e., teaching, scholarship, and service) based on "specific and detailed comments on the performance of the faculty member." When a determination has been made, the dean, committee, and professor sit down and review the documentation and decision.

Tenure. Tenured professors are held accountable at all times; the expectation is for service, scholarship, and grant work to continue. According to a joint 2015 National Education Association (NEA) and American Federation of Teachers (AFT) survey, tenured faculty typically publish more often than their non-tenured peers, serve on more college and university committees, and work approximately 52 hours per week. A professor who wishes to receive tenure must complete a dossier replete with a curriculum vitae (CV), letters of recommendation from sources within and outside the college or university concerning the professor's teaching and service, evidence of publications and presentations, information regarding grants and awards received, and possibly other items depending on the specific institution's standards (AIC 2016; Middlebury College 2016; University of Washington 2012). Each college or university has its own system to confer tenure; however, all institutions have some variation of a multistep committee review, a dean review, and a recommendation to the president, chancellor, or provost (AIC 2016; University of Colorado Office of Policy and Efficiency 2014).

Prior to receiving tenure, a professor can be let go at any time without cause. However, after a professor is tenured, a college or university must prove just cause to fire; thus, tenure becomes the vehicle to due process for professors (NEA and AFT 2015). The NEA and AFT (2015) report that nationally approximately 2% of tenured staff are dismissed each year. An institution must clearly show that the professor under investigation behaved unprofessionally or was incompetent or that perhaps the program or department needed to be closed. Because "tenure is an 'up-or-out' process" (NEA and AFT 2015, n.p.), when professors are denied tenure, they lose their jobs. Although a professor who is denied tenure may be able to file a grievance for reconsideration, such decisions are rarely overturned (Saltzman 2008; University of Colorado Office of Policy and Efficiency 2014). Obviously, the goal for both the postsecondary institution and the professor is to prevent a dismissal from occurring.

Conclusion

Traditionally, the professor's role was to teach and mentor. As this role evolves in the twenty-first century and as professors have the option to be tenured or not, it is important to understand the steps necessary for receiving tenure. An adjunct's first foray into the professoriate often requires long hours for little pay, and the role might include the same additional requirements—beyond teaching and mentoring students—as a tenured professor (Bonetta 2011; Hall 2015). An adjunct must decide if he or she wishes to move into a tenure-track position or remain a non-tenured professor.

The professor who attempts to navigate academia in search of tenure is required to participate in a multifaceted approach that includes excellence in teaching; service within the institution and local community; and scholarship through research, writing, and grants. This three-pronged approach, along with yearly evaluations, creates the necessary conditions by which a professor can then apply for tenure after having completed stints as both an associate professor and an assistant professor (Plater 2008). It is critically important that the prospective professor's dossier includes substantial evidence from all three categories as well as letters of recommendation. After the panel review and final confirmation are complete, a tenured professor must continue to demonstrate progress in teaching, scholarship, and service as long as he or she remains at the institution.

Points to Remember

- Professors have the option of pursuing the tenure track or not; those who choose to bypass the tenure track settle for no advancement or guaranteed job, but they may receive the same title.
- Adjunct teaching is a first step, often accompanied by lower wages, longer hours, and less stature within the teaching community.
- The triad of excellence in teaching, service to institution and community, and extensive scholarship is the surest way to a tenure-track position.
- Tenure is not guaranteed and is only considered by an institution after a professor spends time as an adjunct, associate, and assistant professor.

- The tenure process itself is arduous. A professor must carefully craft his or her dossier from day one, making sure to include a curriculum vitae, publications and presentations, proof of grants and awards, evidence of service, and letters of recommendation from both college personnel and community representatives.

- The college or university considering a professor for tenure uses a multistep process to evaluate a prospective candidate that includes several committee reviews prior to being recommended to the president, provost, or chancellor.

References

Albertine, S. 2013. Toward the next century of leadership: A future faculty model. *Peer Review: The Changing Nature of Faculty Roles* 15(3). Retrieved from https://www.aacu.org/peerreview/2013/summer/albertine

American International College. 2016. Performance review package. Springfield, MA: Author.

Bonetta, L. 2011, February 11. Moving up the academic ladder. *Science.* Retrieved from www.sciencemag.org/careers/features/2011/02/moving_academic_ladder

Coalition on the Academic Workforce. 2012, June. A portrait of part-time faculty members: A summary of findings on part-time faculty respondents to the Coalition on the Academic Workforce survey of contingent faculty members and instructors. Retrieved from http://www.academicworkforce.org/CAW_portrait_2012.pdf

Concordia University. 2015. How to become an adjunct professor: Job, education, salary. Retrieved from http://education.cu-portland.edu/blog/teaching-careers/adjunct-professor/#duties

Curry, T. H. 2006. Faculty performance reviews. *Tomorrow's Professor Postings.* Stanford, CA: Stanford University. Retrieved from https://tomprof.stanford.edu/posting/740

Dakota State University. 2016. Standards document. Madison, SD: Author. Retrieved from https://dsu.edu/assets/uploads/policies/02-45-00.pdf

Hackmann, D. G., and M.M. McCarthy. 2013. What constitutes a critical mass? An investigation of faculty staffing patterns in educational leadership programs. *Journal of Research on Leadership Education* 8(1): 5–27.

Hall, L. 2015, June 22. I am an adjunct professor who teaches five classes. I earn less than a professional pet sitter. *The Guardian.* Retrieved from https://www.theguardian.com/commentisfree/2015/jun/22/adjunct-professor-earn-less-than-pet-sitter

Kezar, A. 2012, November/December. Spanning the great divide between tenure-track and non-tenure track. *Faculty Change: The Magazine of Higher Learning* 44(6). Retrieved from http://www.changemag.org/Archives/Back%20Issues/2012/November-December%202012/spanning-the-great-divide-full.html

Middlebury College. 2016, July 21. Rules of appointment and tenure for academic faculty. *Faculty Handbook*. Middlebury, VT: Author. Retrieved from http://www.middlebury.edu/about/handbook/faculty/Faculty_Rules

National Education Association and American Federation of Teachers. 2015. The truth about tenure in higher education. Retrieved from http://www.nea.org/home/33067.htm

Oregon State University. 2015, June 11. Criteria for promotion and tenure. *Faculty Handbook: Promotion and Tenure Guidelines*. Corvallis, OR: Author. Retrieved from http://oregonstate.edu/admin/aa/faculty-handbook-promotion-and-tenure-guidelines%23waiver#criteria

Plater, W. M. 2008. The twenty-first-century professoriate. *Academe* 94(4): 35–40.

Roney, K., and S.L. Ulerick. 2013. A roadmap to engaging part-time faculty in high-impact practices. *Peer Review: The Changing Nature of Faculty Roles* 15(3). Retrieved from https://www.aacu.org/peerreview/2013/summer/roney-ulerick

Saltzman, G. M. 2008. Dismissals, layoffs, and tenure denials in colleges and universities. In *The NEA 2008 almanac of higher education* (pp. 51–66). Washington, DC: National Education Association. Retrieved from http://www.nea.org/assets/img/PubAlmanac/ALM_08_05.pdf

University of Colorado Office of Policy and Efficiency. 2014. Administrative policy statement: Standards, processes, and procedures for comprehensive review, tenure, post-tenure review and promotion. Retrieved from https://www.cu.edu/ope/aps/1022

University of Washington Dean's Office, College of Arts and Sciences. 2012. Promotion to full professor guidelines. Retrieved from https://admin.artsci.washington.edu/promotion-full-professor-guidelines

University of Washington Rules Coordination Office. 2016. Appointment and promotion of faculty members. *Faculty Code and Governance. UW Policy Directory*. Retrieved from http://www.washington.edu/admin/rules/policies/FCG/FCCH24.html

Uzuner-Smith, S. and K. Englander. 2015. Exposing ideology within university policies: A critical discourse analysis of faculty hiring, promotion, and remuneration practices. *Journal of Education Policy* 30(1): 62-85.

CHAPTER 2

Connections in the Classroom
The Faculty Member's Role in Relational Retention

By Christine N. Michael

Introduction

Most young people in American society today hope to go to college, but many face formidable barriers. Historically, students from low-income families, students of color, and students with disabilities have had limited access to resources that will promote college access (Davis 2010). Many attend schools that lack rigorous college preparation programs. As a result, few graduate from high school ready for college success. In addition, first-generation students often do not have family members who can act in the guidance role as they transition from community of origin to the college campus; this fact alone jeopardizes their chances of success even if they are accepted into a college or university (Engle and Tinto 2008).

Approximately 55% of first-time/full-time students will complete their bachelor's degree within six years, yet only 11% of first-generation, low-income students will do so (Engle and Tinto 2008). While access for low-income, first-generation students has increased, successful completion of a college degree, especially an undergraduate degree, has not (Engle and Tinto 2008). Low-income, first-generation students are four times more likely to leave college after their first year than those without these risk factors, and six years later, 43% of them had left without any degree attainment (Engle and Tinto 2008). These statistics are particularly troublesome, given that at this point in history, first-generation college students comprise nearly one-third of all matriculated undergraduates (Institute for Higher Education Policy [IHEP] 2012).

Even those who persist are likely to earn lower grades, need more developmental courses, take fewer credits (and thus take longer to graduate), withdraw from more courses, and need more ancillary academic assistance than their nonfirst-generation peers (IHEP 2012). First-generation students are more likely to be financially independent, come from low-income backgrounds, and have dependents; they also tend to enroll part-time, work more than 40 hours per week, rely on more federal Pell grants, and attend public two-year or for-profit institutions (IHEP 2012). As IHEP (2012, 6) reports, "all of these characteristics are shown to be negatively correlated with college enrollment and persistence to a post-secondary degree."

For the purpose of this chapter, first-generation college students are defined as students who do not have a parent who has attended college. First-generation students who are also students of color or members of minority groups experience their own additional sets of challenges. As Watson, Terrell, and Wright (2002, 7-8) point out, "On predominantly White campuses, many minority students experience a climate of widespread distrust and victimization. A large number of White students believe that students of color receive special privileges such as lower admissions standards, compensatory education, support programs, scholarships, and employment opportunities not afforded to them." Terrell and Wright also express concern over the low numbers of faculty of color who might serve additionally as mentors. Tinto (1993, 186) shares this concern but notes nonetheless that "the retention of students of color, as it is for students generally, is everyone's responsibility."

In addition to the crushing sense of personal failure, students who do not persist to graduation also are likely to end up with substantial debt. In attempts to address issues of transitioning from secondary school to higher education, colleges and universities have focused on academic advising, financial aid advising, and residence life counseling. However, findings from this chapter author's original qualitative research with underserved students indicate that relationships and interpersonal issues, such as renegotiating roles with family, friends, and home community, are the most critical variables in whether they can successfully navigate the transition or not (Michael and Wilkins 2013). In their interviews, students from this demographic expressed the power that mentors—peer, academic, staff, and other—have had in helping them build the relational resiliency that has allowed them to cultivate positive relationships that supported their academic goals and renegotiate or jettison relationships that hindered them.

There is no lack of scholarly literature on the transition to college and college retention. Much of it, however, focuses on academic preparedness and the cognitive realm. But what does research tell us about the roles of the psychological and social domains in successful persistence to graduation? The ACT (2004) study of college retention found that social support and social involvement on campus were as important in retention to graduation as high school grade point average; these factors were even more important than ACT assessment scores. Despite poor academic performance, many college students persist because of their successful social integration and feelings of fit within their institution. Such social integration is especially important for students who are first-generation college attendees, have limited English proficiency, or are from a cultural or minority background. The 2004 ACT study also concluded that one of the major factors influencing college retention is that each student has a quality relationship with at least one concerned person on campus. Michael and Wilkins (2013, 28), based on their interviews with first-generation college students who had successfully persisted to graduation, coined the phrase "relational retention," which is "the intentional use of positive personal relationships to increase the likelihood of persistence to graduation." Faculty, Michael and Wilkins (2013) concluded, are able to play a powerful role in relational retention, if they choose to see this as part of their role.

The aforementioned data suggest that it is no longer a matter of choice whether professors see themselves in a newly defined role, but that it is a matter of vital necessity if they are to aid in the true mission of a college education: developing each student's unique capacities. The new professoriate cannot be the proverbial "sage on the stage," the deliverer of content knowledge only; his or her expanded role includes developing and nurturing the relationships with students that lie at the heart of transformative learning.

Relationships Matter

Bean and Eaton (2001) discovered that students who were "socially integrated" rather than "socially avoidant" experienced feelings of connectedness on campus that fed back into their positive psychological assessments of their own self-efficacy, ability to handle stressors, and internal locus of control. The more they were integrated into the life of the college, the greater their experience of personal competence and efficacy. Campus-based relationships, it seems, can be social buffers against stress. This perception is confirmed in the work of Harper and Quaye (2009) and Jehangir (2010).

Jehangir (2010) noted that faculty and staff have a critical part to play in helping first-generation college students persist and thrive during their first year of college. Students reported that they deeply valued instances in which there was a departure from the typical "teacher-student" role. They praised classrooms and other learning environments in which faculty modeled genuine caring about their students, and the students, in turn, learned to care about one another's success.

Jehangir's participants talked about the importance of both faculty and their peers being advocates for them as they struggled to assimilate into campus life. When they felt that faculty cared about them as unique individuals, they felt more tightly connected to the campus culture and more likely to persist to graduation. They also valued situations in which they saw faculty members truly invested in learning about them as people and about their cultures and backgrounds, rather than faculty seeing themselves as the repositories of all knowledge.

Martinez, Sher, Krull, and Wood (2009) report similar findings; however, they note that first-generation students are much less likely to be involved in campus life than are their non-first-generation counterparts. This is a distressing finding, given that the researchers also discovered that first-generation students derived greater outcome benefits from extracurricular involvement and peer interaction when these took place. Stuber (2011) concurs, noting that first-generation college students participate in fewer extracurricular activities, athletics, and volunteer opportunities. Such activities are the pathways to new communities of peers and mentors with similar interests, and they may also yield contacts that are useful in internship, campus work, and career transitions.

In their book, *College of the Overwhelmed*, Kadison and DiGeronimo (2004, 10) highlight the issue of identity development in college, particularly during the first year. They write that often "young adults cling to family values and beliefs for security, but on some deeper level they realize that not all of the old values and beliefs fit anymore. This pull of loyalties can cause great personal discomfort." This pull can be particularly painful for first-generation college students, whose cultural backgrounds frequently do not parallel the dominant values or beliefs expressed on majority campuses.

In many students' cases, they may be criticized for spending their time focused on their education rather than with friends and family. Feelings of resentment may grow and become exacerbated even more if these significant individuals perceive that their student if pulling away from their culture in favor of the different dominant culture of campus:

> First-generation students often sense displeasure on the part of acquaintances and feel an uncomfortable separation from the culture in which they grew up. Such tensions frequently require students to negotiate relationships with friends and relatives, something that is not easy to do and does not always have a happy ending. (Ward, Siegel, and Davenport 2012, 73)

Ward et al. (2012) discuss the idea of "cultural capital," or the information and beliefs a student needs to succeed in the college environment. While parents of first-generation students obviously want their children to do well, they themselves do not possess the cultural capital specific to higher education to pass along to their children. Thus, their children lack "the information, familiarity, jargon, cultural understanding, experience, and emotional bearings that the students need to effectively tackle the challenge of the college environment" (Ward et al. 2012, 7).

The previously cited ACT (2004) study called for the creation of activities and programs that intentionally facilitate the building of social and learning communities and use faculty, staff, and student mentors to be the conduit of cultural capital that may be lacking when first-generation students arrive on campus. The study's authors hailed programs and academic courses that build mentoring and support groups into their fabric as powerful agents in increasing students' motivation, self-confidence, and engagement on campus. At the center of many of these strategies are caring professors who define their roles beyond transmitters of content knowledge to transformers of young lives.

Retention as a Faculty Role

Tinto (1993) concluded that failure to negotiate rites of passage—separating from family, high school, and local community and forming a new identity, friends, and a community with similar values—was key in students' dropping out of college. Tinto (2000) later expanded his own model to include even greater emphasis on "linking learning and leaving," arguing for building supportive peer groups through first-year learning communities so that each first-year student could develop a small group of early friends. Saying that "academic and social systems are two nested spheres," Tinto (2000, 91) stresses the need for "bringing faculty back into the theory of student persistence." Tinto draws a direct correlation between student persistence and "student-faculty contact outside the classroom.… This relationship is likely to mirror how faculty actions shape student experiences within the classroom and, in turn, student willingness to seek out faculty beyond the classroom" (2000, 90–91). Student engagement with faculty, Tinto (2000) found, is linked to students' willingness to seek out those faculty and other student peers outside of the classroom regarding their learning issues. Such engagement improves the quality of their learning. They also are more likely "to develop values stressing the importance of involvement with others" (Tinto 2000, 69). This stance, Tinto discovered, predicts future involvement and "is associated with heightened intellectual and social development" (2000, 69–70). This holds true even when factors such as prior level of development, ability levels, and prior educational experience are considered. What Tinto (2000, 71) uncovered is simple yet powerful: "Student contact with faculty, especially outside of class, is critical to student success." He remarks that interactions with faculty can occur in both formal and informal settings, and both lead to enhanced intellectual development; with that development comes enhanced "integration into the academic system of the college" (Tinto 2000, 118). With this greater integration, first-generation students gain "greater exposure … to the multiple dimensions of academic work" (Tinto 2000, 118). This exposure begins to level the playing field as far as "college knowledge" that nonfirst-generation students possess upon their arrival.

First-generation college students need personal relationships with faculty and staff: "The symbolic impact of being able to say, 'I know Professor Smith' cannot be underestimated" (Davis 2010, 197). Because underserved populations often suffer from what Davis (2010) calls the "imposter syndrome," validation by faculty and staff on campus becomes a critical variable in resiliency and retention. Faculty mentors, according to Davis (2010, 79), must broaden their role to build relational resiliency in fragile students. Furthermore, this author writes that "no one should be surprised that achieving a personal relationship with a faculty member is one of the strongest markers for academic success for students who are the first in their family to attend college." Filkins and Doyle (2002 as cited in Davis 2010) note that first-generation students are often hyperaware of their academic deficiencies and may avoid seeking out social contact with faculty. "The frequency and nature of student-faculty interactions have the greatest impact when they focus on topics that engage students on an intellectual level in contrast to an exclusively social level" (Filkins and Doyle 2002, 80). This finding emphasizes the importance of the classroom as a place for first-generation students to grow both academically and personally.

Bean stresses the importance not only of connection to the institution but of the sense of academic self-efficacy that a student must possess if he or she is to persist to graduation. A large part of self-efficacy must be rooted in the classroom experience, where the student "develops the sense of academic self-efficacy, approaches academic work, develops an internal locus of control related to academic achievement, gets good grades, feels loyal to the school, and chooses to continue enrollment there" (2005, 227). Clearly, faculty members are at the very center of this process.

Upcraft, Gardner, and Barefoot acknowledge that "some faculty members maintain a restricted view of their role as educators. This view appears with some variation on the general theme that first-year issues are beyond the scope of faculty matters. One variation on this theme is that retention issues are the purview of administration and student affairs personnel" (2005, 200). Upcraft et al. go on to remark that such faculty see developmental education, remediation, co-curricular matters, and interpersonal relationships with students as "not part of the job description" (2005, 200). Administration and faculty leadership must provide both ethical and financial arguments, rooted in research on the importance of faculty-student connections, against these narrow role descriptions.

The scholarly literature and research cited here demonstrate the necessity of beginning a dialogue and taking steps to redefine the professoriate. While some faculty members continue to argue that their role and training should not be confused with that of a counselor, it behooves those who come into contact with college students in and out of the classroom to embrace tenets of relational education, mentoring, and human potential development within the parameters of their job descriptions.

What Students Say They Need: Case Studies

Juan. This chapter author's own research provides poignant illustrations that will serve to underscore the importance of relational education. For example, "Juan," a first-generation, low-income student of Dominican descent who graduated from a low-performing public high school in New York City, remembers how crucial mentoring—in several different forms —was to his success as an undergraduate. "When I arrived on campus," he recalled, "I really needed mentors. This was a whole new territory, and I was wide open to getting as much mentoring as I could." In addition to being academically unprepared for college, "no one in my home culture could really help me." Three professors in particular "identified resources for me, which eventually led me into student government and study abroad. I got invited to go to conferences with them; they helped me get scholarships; and I chose my major of anthropology because of one of them, who was a man of color and someone I wanted to be."

This one professor, who became Juan's academic advisor and primary mentor, went so far as to invite him to become the babysitter for his children. In reaching out to create a new family structure for Juan, the professor filled a huge emotional void by providing a warm home environment in which Juan was seen as another member of the family. In that setting, as Juan relates, "I began to see an image of a life that I wanted to have, both with other people and in the life of the mind. I had heard that phrase before, but I never really understood what it meant." As he became more secure in the psychological domain, Juan began to accept more challenges academically. In addition to taking more difficult classes, applying for scholarships, studying abroad, and co-presenting at conferences, Juan ran for class office and became the president of the student government—no small feat given that he was one of only a handful of students of color on campus.

Faculty who taught in the learning community model were essential in helping Juan and other first-generation students learn how to enter the academic tradition. Relationships with others on campus helped Juan to transition from his home community in a way that promoted personal and academic growth:

> There was a lot of emphasis on relationships, especially in the learning communities. That's key for first-generation [students], to help them develop a professional style of conversation and also to be able to maintain their values and traditions from where they came from. Those relationships helped me bridge the gap between higher education and lack of education. The bridge allowed me to maintain my pride and also forge a new identity, not forgetting the place I came from. It made me appreciate my own success so that I didn't feel guilty about getting out.

A sense of impostership and guilt over leaving friends and family behind commonly attend first-generation students, and one can see from

Juan's story that caring faculty are crucial in students' successful negotiation of these feelings.

Stephanie. Seemingly worlds away, Stephanie, who grew up in the rural Adirondack Mountains of New York and attended a pre-K–12 public school whose total population was 190 students, also faced transitional issues. The salient challenges of her first term included being "homesick so much. I missed the way my old teachers were, how they knew about me, knew who I was." Entering a challenging nursing program at a college a distance from her home, Stephanie initially floundered, calling her parents and pleading hysterically for them to pick her up and take her back. Fortunately, her first-semester English professor stepped into a mentoring role and supported Stephanie through her initial challenges: "She had been a principal in a small town, and she was just what I was looking for. I got really close to her. She would actually talk with [students] one-to-one and listened to us express our feelings. Even though the course was Research and Rhetoric, she let us use the writing as a way to work through our issues."

Stephanie was also lost as to how to tackle the ramped-up academic requirements at college:

> My RA really noticed that after the first few weeks, when I would go around knocking on everyone's door and introducing myself, I kept my door shut and really didn't socialize. I thought that was how I had to study because I was struggling with the work so much in the beginning. She suggested that I leave the door open, study in an environment where other people were around, and I learned that I didn't have to be so closed in and alone so much.

Stephanie's faculty advisor reinforced the value of interconnected learning, suggesting that the nursing students form their own study groups. This suggestion was instrumental in helping Stephanie succeed:

> Nursing is very competitive and very hard, so it's hard to have a social life. My peers are not my best friends, but they're like my coworkers or professional colleagues. We do study groups together and, every Thursday, we will have dinner together after 10 hours of clinical work. It doesn't take the place of family, but it's the support like a professional network.

Tito. Tito, Colombian born, adopted and raised in New York City, became embroiled in drug issues and gang activities while in secondary school; his brothers then moved him to a small, rural town in upstate New York where he thrived as a student, school leader, and community member. However, after being accepted at a large, state university, Tito quickly found himself enmeshed in a new round of problems.

Among the challenges of his first year as a first-generation student were building positive relationships, fitting into the campus culture, and avoiding drug problems that had plagued him in high school. Tito explained, "I got into trouble in the summer, got involved with the wrong people, tried harder drugs, and got into that lifestyle." Arriving on a sprawling urban campus in the capital city of New York, Tito floundered:

> I was not into any extracurricular activities in the first year. I was unprepared for Greek life and the relationship with folks selling drugs on campus. . . . I went on a free-for-all and got back involved with my old behaviors.

Eventually, Tito wound up on the wrong side of the law, which led him, in strange ways, to the connections that would help him shine on campus. The first was the district attorney handling his drug case. "I had to face reality. I could have gotten 1–9 years in a state penitentiary, but he gave me 60 days instead, and a rehabilitation program instead of time. He cleaned up my life by assigning me a faculty mentor who was there to refer me, work with the system, and get me involved in campus programs."

Tito also "clicked" with his faculty advisor, after he decided that rather than become a problem within legal and governmental systems, he wanted to study and pursue a career in those fields. "[My faculty advisor] provided openness, honesty, friendship by asking lots of active questions, like 'How's life?' and really listening no matter what you said. He actually went out of his way and was speaking with my family."

Tito was recommended to enter a living-learning community in which students shared a dormitory with peers and professors and took their classes within their living environment. Tito explained, "I was able to be in a situation where I could live and learn on the same floor. My professor was there, and he went above and beyond to treat you like a friend. I was looked upon as a young scholar who deserves to have an adult conversation." As with Juan, Tito not only thrived as a student but also earned coveted spots in student government organizations, majoring in political science, and serving in various change agency roles at the university.

Relational retention efforts additionally require that mentors strengthen mentees' ability to identify relationships that are barriers to their successful attainment of their goals. In Juan's case, he was helped to learn strategies to distance himself respectfully from peers and family members who were impediments to his learning: "Every family has its own drama, but I had to put that all on the back burner. That's why my mentors and their families were so important." For Stephanie, learning to rise above her mother's level of comfort with her desire to drop out was a key step in her persistence. "When I called home and said, 'Come and get me. I can't do this,' she said 'Come home. It's okay. You can just go to community college here next semester.'" As Stephanie came to rely more on her faculty and peer mentors, she recognized that taking the easy route back to what was familiar would rob her of the chance to grow and change. Tito's telling comment about being treated as "a young scholar" demonstrates the necessity of faculty's viewing even the most initially marginal students on campus as "at promise" rather than "at risk."

What Faculty Can Do

The faculty member's stance. Hao (2011) introduced the idea of "critical compassionate pedagogy" when faculty are working with first-generation college students. Similar in many ways to earlier notions of "holistic education," this stance asks educators to actively examine their standard classroom practices and activities to ensure that they do not assume first-generation students are operating at deficit positions; this stance also requires educators to practice compassion at all times in their interactions with students. Professors operate within and outside of their classrooms as advocates for their first-generation students, and they recognize each of them as a whole human being—both in personal strengths, which are brought to the academic discourse, and in challenges that may be unique to each student.

There are four necessary components to compassionate communication: observation, feeling, need, and request. According to Hao (2011), first-generation college students are too frequently viewed from the "deficits" model; therefore, they are assumed to have greater academic needs and less to contribute to the life of the classroom and campus. By employing the four components of compassionate communication within one's classroom, a skilled faculty member can observe who each student is as a unique learner and individual, recognize the feelings he or she possesses about what will be necessary to successfully work with the first-generation student, choose a pedagogical approach that will address each learner's needs, and request information from the student that will be incorporated into improving learning strategies and environments.

The act of being an ally. Faculty have a powerful role in validating first-generation students' sense that they belong on campus and can succeed in the classroom. As Terenzini, Rendon, Upcraft, Millar, Allison, Gregg, and Jalomo (1994) found, instructor support not only encouraged students to believe that they could succeed, but it instilled an "obligation to succeed" because of their connection to the instructor. Students who took part in Terenzini et al.'s (1994) study identified common characteristics in faculty they considered to be allies: engaging in positive communication, creating a sense of belonging, providing classroom activities that include their life experiences, and being noticeably invested in the students. The IHEP (2012, 9) report describes successful faculty allies as those who are "transforming their roles into stronger champions for first-generation student success."

Faculty who themselves were first-generation are especially positioned to serve as allies and role models. A key component of Ward et al.'s (2012) learning matrix for first-generation students is the involvement of such faculty in mentoring programs, informal dinners, and specially designed seminars and lectures. Yet all faculty can recognize "that [first-generation students] bring a unique yet underrepresented perspective into academia" and can create "a space that is respectful and appreciative of all" (Housel and Harvey 2009, 31). In addition, faculty can connect students with successful first-generation students who can serve as mentors and provide the student's eye view of college life.

Using culturally responsive pedagogy. Harper and Quaye (2009) stress the need to adopt culturally responsive pedagogy in the classroom to more fully integrate first-generation and other underserved populations. In such a model, faculty strive to develop curricula that enable students to grow as individuals and learn more about themselves; this cannot take place in a curriculum whose issues, topics, or materials are not meaningful to students. For first-generation students who are also members of minority groups, "consideration of the language spoken at home, connections to the community, culturally responsive content, and classroom management" are necessary elements (Au 1998, as cited in Harper and Quaye 2009, 162).

Diversity in learning styles based upon cultural preferences and conditioning is another important consideration. While it may seem daunting to address every individual's preferences in every academic assignment—

especially in a large class—monitoring to be certain that there are myriad ways of presenting and assessing course content is certainly possible.

Co-constructing knowledge. Baxter Magolda (2004, as cited in Harper and Quaye 2009) developed the Learning Partnerships Model as a means of engaging marginalized students in predominantly White classrooms, but the tenets are valuable to first-generation students' classroom experiences as well. The professor's role within this model is to "validate students as knowers; encourage students to use their experiences in learning; and mutually construct knowledge with students" (Baxter Magolda 2004, 166–167). Although this model entails faculty giving up their historical role as knowledge "authority figures," the social construction of knowledge that the model affords invites partnerships with their students that respect diversity of experience.

Harper and Quaye quote one of their student participants as he describes the ideal balance of cognate and social knowledge construction: "Make issues related to racial/ethnic minority groups a central part of the curriculum. Engage this type of material as they would engage physics" (2009, 167). While the student acknowledges that a physics professor cannot be expected to spend the majority of his or her class time on literature or the arts related to students' backgrounds, he stresses that the professor can point out contributions to the field by individuals from various ethnic and racial backgrounds. Attention to the dynamics of such variables as social class, gender, religion, and sexual orientation can widen the circle of knowledge construction.

First-generation students themselves note the critical importance of openly discussing issues of class. As Lawless (2009, reviewed in Housel and Harvey 2009) describes in her personal essay, greater sensitivity to the lived experience of low-income students is needed. She cites Dean's (1989, 30) auto-ethnographic account of this phenomenon:

> It was within a traditional course on introductory sociology that I first heard my class background discussed. In that class, 'the working-class experience' was presented as an object to be studied rather than as a possible experiential reality for students in the room. I felt not only invisible, but dehumanized.

Collaborating while learning. Harper and Quaye (2009) see collaborative learning experiences as one of the primary means of promoting success among students. Working cooperatively, rather than competitively, to master course content allows for learning both about the subject at hand as well as about classmates as people. Intercultural competence can be gained when students are encouraged to discuss different ways of approaching knowledge and problem solving. While some institutions offer living-learning communities, where students from the same classes share an actual dormitory with classrooms, the savvy instructor can duplicate many of those experiences through such activities as peer review of writing, sharing reflections and personal insights, and discussing the ways in which different cultures construct and value knowledge. "By exchanging knowledge, students begin to develop an appreciation for others, which can translate into an acceptance of differences" (Harper and Quaye 2009, 171).

Serving others while learning. Upcraft et al. (2005) are strong proponents of service learning as a powerful tool in first-generation college student acculturation on campus. Because this form of learning is mentored, hands-on, applied, and community-based, it engages first-generation students through research-based strengths of their own. The aforementioned authors (2005) note that first-generation students may have little knowledge or unrealistic ideas about career and academic major choices. For example, many students gravitate toward the business major because they believe that it is lucrative rather than making the choice based on personal interests or "goodness of fit." They also may enter college in Marcia's (1980) stage of "foreclosure," or mere acceptance of one's career path based upon what others have told them rather than self-scrutiny and individualized choice based on prior experience.

McKay and Estrella (2008) found that the quality of interaction with faculty is directly correlated with how first-generation students perceive their efficacy in accomplishing short- and long-term goals. Students reported that discussions about the content of the course, their experiences during service learning, and their reflections on what they had learned about themselves during the experiences were vital in promoting personal growth. This sense of greater competence, confidence, and social connection, in turn, promoted a greater likelihood of persistence. Service and other forms of experiential learning directly support the preferred learning styles of newly entering college students.

According to Upcraft et al., 60% of entering students prefer learning styles "characterized by a preference for direct, concrete experience; moderate to high degrees of structure; linear, sequential learning; and often the need to know why before doing something"; at the same time, however, 75% of faculty prefer global styles of teaching, rooted in the worlds of concepts, ideas, and abstractions, and assume that students need "a high degree of autonomy in their work" (2005, 362). Heeding these findings, even faculty who are not teaching service-learning or experiential courses can adapt their teaching styles to the needs of newly entering first-generation students; in fact, these approaches will assist most new students.

Active involvement in the classroom. To invite first-generation students into the academic tradition, wise faculty who teach first-year classes will use multiple techniques to connect students to the curriculum and to one another. Among these are small group discussions, "writing-to-learn" activities, case studies and scenarios, and problem-based learning (Upcraft et al. 2005). Small group discussions offer opportunities for all students to participate actively, which may be especially difficult if they are enrolled in large classes. Study groups, project groups, and class groups that remain consistent throughout the term build relationships among students and also expose them to diversity in opinions, backgrounds, and learning styles.

Writing activities can be employed in different ways, beyond the traditional use of writing assignments to assess what students know. In writing-to-learn activities, the purpose is to have students write to capture their thoughts and views, reflect upon them, and potentially revise them. Not only does writing help students better understand their texts (Bean 2005), it also helps them better know themselves. Further, this approach accommodates students who prefer thinking things through prior to engaging in discussion or other class activities.

Case studies (which tell stories) and scenarios (which present situations) value the life experiences that first-generation students bring to the classroom and expose students to diverse approaches to solving the same problem. Indeed, any kind of problem-based learning tends to appeal to students because it "literally turns instruction around. Instead of teaching students what they need to know and then posing problems or cases in which students explore implications and applications, PBL approaches begin with the problem, and the problem drives what students learn and in what order" (Upcraft et al. 2005, 253). Used within learning groups that stay together throughout the term, problem-based learning draws on skills that most first-generation students already possess; to overcome obstacles and gain access to postsecondary education, they have already proven themselves as adept problem-solvers in the real world.

Umbach and Wawrzynski (2005) relate similar findings to those mentioned previously. In their study using two national data sets to explore the connection between student engagement and faculty practices, students reported greater engagement and learning when faculty interact with their students, challenge them to higher academic achievement, employ active and collaborative learning techniques, stress higher-order thinking activities, and value other kinds of enriching educational experiences.

Promoting peer connections. Skillful instructors can use their classrooms in ways that connect first-generation students with peers, especially if they are not involved in formal living-learning types of situations. Davis (2010) found that while instructors assumed that students would seek one another out for academic support, many had no experience in doing so; first-generation students, he found, need to be placed in study groups, as they often do not perceive the need to be in them, nor do they have the confidence to form one. Pointing new students toward others who can mentor—informally or formally—can help bolster their acculturation. Creating panels or opportunities for more veteran first-generation students to share their experiences may lessen the "imposter syndrome" (Davis 2010, 186). It behooves professors to see their role as including some of the characteristics of a host or hostess on campus, introducing students to others who have walked their path as well as to those who have experiences that are divergent from their own. As Harper and Quaye (2009, 6) succinctly put it, "Weak institutions are those that expect students to engage themselves." Further, "an erroneous assumption is often made that students will naturally learn about their peers simply by coming into contact" (Harper and Quaye 2009, 7). Instead, Harper and Quaye argue that the campus must be committed to facilitating engagements, and "educators must facilitate structured opportunities for dialogues to transpire" (2009, 7).

Advancing academic advising. Faculty members for whom academic advising is a formal part of their role must realize that most first-generation students will need specialized academic advising. Davis (2010) summarizes studies showing that first-generation students take longer choosing their major and make choices based upon different criteria than their non-first-generation counterparts. These criteria may not necessarily lead to "goodness of fit" between the student and his or her academic concentration. Often, choices are made out of perceived fiscal necessity and the beliefs that certain majors lead to better salaries that can support students and their families. When concentration choices do not fit a student's interests and talents, he or she often must eventually abandon the major, thus taking more time and spending more money to graduate.

Academic advisors also can play a powerful role in integrating first-generation students into campus life. "Academic advisors can use some of their time with students to explain the advantages of engagement and encouraging them to become involved with peers in campus events and organizations and invest effort in educational activities known to promote student learning and development" (Harper and Quaye 2009, 316).

Because students may be reluctant to take advantage of advisors' office hours and because once-a-term meetings may not be sufficient, many colleges and universities with high populations of first-generation students are resorting to mandatory, regular advisory meetings. They also are hiring more advisors and avoiding the cost-savings tendency of using those outside of the academic disciplines in advisory roles.

What Institutions Can Do

The 2012 IHEP report identifies three key strategies to support faculty as they transition from "knowledge disseminators" to the value-added role of "key ally" to first-generation students. The first step involves augmenting existing and developing new opportunities for faculty to work in collaboration with first-generation students. This is particularly effective when cross-disciplinary collaborations exist, inviting students to understand how knowledge is constructed from various disciplinary lenses. A second approach is to formalize and reinforce "changes to faculty roles as related to student success" (IHEP 2012, 10). This strategy requires "explicit language to support first-generation students in faculty position descriptions," recognition of this effort in annual faculty performance reviews, and public recognition or incentives for effectively working with this population (IHEP 2012, 11). At institutions where "publish-or-perish" and research requirements overshadow teaching and mentoring, new emphasis must be placed on the value of this role shift for the professoriate.

A third recommendation of the IHEP (2012) report centers on engaging faculty in the academic disciplines and departments whose courses pose the greatest challenges to first-generation students. As these learners tend to need more developmental courses in mathematics and English than their non-first-generation peers, such students can benefit from faculty efforts to revitalize the curriculum in these and STEM courses.

Harper and Quaye (2009) reaffirm these suggestions and also call for greater funding of faculty development and research related to success with first-generation students. They find that faculty also need coaching in learning how to set clear expectations for classrooms that are respectful of all members:

> When students share perspectives that are harmful to others, faculty members should address those comments immediately. However, it is equally important for faculty not to silence those who share controversial ideas. This tricky balance can be managed through creating classroom settings that respect differences. For example, White students should be invited to understand their privilege and be able to work through their own anxieties in classroom settings. (Harper and Quaye 2009, 173)

For most professors, such skills in classroom management have not been an explicit part of their graduate training.

Harper and Quaye (2009) further suggest that faculty participate in professional development aimed at creating rich and diverse curricula. This can be achieved, in part, through collaborative peer review of course syllabi, where faculty review one another's syllabi to determine the degree of diversity represented in the assignments and viewpoints that undergird their courses.

Obviously, meaningful professional development in the aforementioned areas is required, as are new ways of measuring faculty and student success in the classroom. In addition, it is not surprising that Housel and Harvey (2009) entitled their book *The Invisibility Factor*. Although they share stories of students' sense of invisibility on campus, first-generation faculty members are also often nonexistent or invisible. Some of the most powerful professional development may come in the form of current faculty listening to the poignant personal reflections of both first-generation undergraduate students and first-generation professors who have successfully navigated college life.

Conclusion

Faculty are key to relational retention. By intentionally increasing the number of first-generation and other underserved students who have meaningful relationships with people while at college, institutions of higher education can significantly increase the probability of these students successfully persisting to graduation. By doing so, more of them will be in a position to fulfill their potential and create a new generation of students who assume that postsecondary education is part of their birthright and who feel adequately prepared and supported by faculty and staff at higher education institutions to attain their academic goals. This shift in the way professors think about their roles can usher in a new definition of the professoriate—one that moves beyond just the dissemination of content knowledge and skills, to one that embraces the relevance and richness of being in relationship with the students whom they serve.

Points to Remember

- Professors are key factors in the retention of students, particularly first-generation students.
- Faculty members must define their roles to go beyond transmitters of academic knowledge to transformers of young lives.
- Although most professors have been trained in their specific academic discipline, many have not been educated in stances, pedagogies, and classroom interactions that may best support first-generation students.
- Institutions of higher education have a responsibility to provide clear role definitions, professional development, support, and recognition to those who work with first-generation students.
- Academic advisors may need professional development on the specialized advising that first-generation students require.
- Active engagement in the classroom, through various experiences, best engages first-generation students.
- Faculty can play a powerful role in helping first-generation students integrate into the campus through clubs, peer relationships, and activities proven to promote student learning.
- First-generation students should be encouraged to serve as resources to newer first-generation students through mentoring, role modeling, advising, and leading clubs and study groups.

References

ACT Policy Report 2004. The role of academic and non-academic factors in improving college retention. ERIC Document # ED485476.

Au. K. 1998. Social constructivism and the school literacy learning of students of diverse backgrounds. *Journal of Literacy Research* 30 (2): 297-319.

Baxter Magolda, M.B. and P.M. King. 2004. Learning partnership model: A framework for promoting self-authorship. In *Learning partnerships: Theory and models of practice to educate for self-authorship* (pp. 37-62), edited by M.B. Baxter Magolda and P.M. King. Sterling, VA: Stylus.

Bean, J. P. 1996. *Engaging ideas: The professor's guide to integrating writing, critical thinking, and active learning in the classroom.* San Francisco, CA: Jossey-Bass.

Bean, J. P. 2005. Nine themes of college student retention. In *College student retention: Formula for student success* (pp. 215–244), edited by A. Seidman. Westport, CT: ACE/Praeger.

Bean, J. P., and Eaton, S. B. 2001. The psychology underlying successful retention practices. *Journal of College Student Retention* 3(1): 73–89.

Davis, J. 2010. *The first-generation student experience: Implications for campus practice and strategies for improving persistence and success.* Sterling, VA: Stylus.

Engle, J., and V. Tinto. 2008. *Moving beyond access: College success for low-income, first-generation students.* Washington, DC: Pell Institute for the Study of Opportunity in Education.

Filkins and Doyle. 2002. *First generation and low income students: Using the NSSE data to study effective educational practice and students' self-reported gains.* Paper presented at the 2002 Association for Institutional Research Annual Conference, Toronto, Ontario, Canada.

Hao, R. N. 2011, September 16. Critical compassionate pedagogy and the teacher's role in first-generation student success. *New Directions for Teaching and Learning* Fall (127): 91–98.

Harper, S., and S.J. Quaye, eds. 2009. *tudent engagement in higher education: Theoretical and practical approaches for diverse populations.* New York, NY: Routledge.

Housel, H., and V. Harvey. 2009. *The invisibility factor: Administrators and faculty reach out to first-generation college students.* Boca Raton, FL: Brown-Walker Press.

Institute for Higher Education Policy. 2012, September. *Issue brief: Supporting first-generation college students through classroom-based practices.* Washington, DC: IHEP.

Jehangir, R. R. 2010. *Higher education and first-generation students: Cultivating community, voice, and place for the new majority.* New York, NY: Palgrave Macmillan.

Kadison, R., and T.F. DiGeronimo. 2004. *College of the overwhelmed: The campus mental health crisis and what to do about it.* San Francisco, CA: Jossey-Bass.

Lawless, B. 2009. Guiding class consciousness in first-generation college students: A pragmatic approach to classism in the academy. In *The invisibility factor: Administrators and faculty reach out to first-generation college students,* edited by T.H. and V.L. Harvey. Boca Raton, FL: BrownWalker Press.

Marcia, J.E. 1980. Identity in adolescence. *Handbook of Adolescent Psychology* 9 (11): 159-187.

Martinez, J.A., K.J. Sher, J.L. Krull, and P.K. Wood. 2009. Blue-collar scholars?: Mediators and moderators of university attrition in first-generation college students. *Journal of College Student Development* 50(1): 87-103.

McKay, V.C. and J. Estrella. 2008. First-generation student success: The role of faculty interaction in service learning courses. *Journal of Communication Education* 57(3): 356-372.

Michael, C., and V. Wilkins. 2013, January 14. *Relational retention: Connections that keep students on campus.* Presentation given at Higher Education Teaching and Learning (HETL) Association Conference, University of Central Florida, Orlando, FL.

Stuber, J.M. 2011. Integrated, marginal and resilient: race, class and the diverse experiences of white first-generation college students. *International Journal of Qualitative Studies in Education* 24(1): 117-136. http://dx.doi.org/10.1080/09518391003641916

Terenzini, P. T., L.I. Rendon, M.L. Upcraft, J. Millar, K. Allison, P. Gregg, and R. Jalomo. 1994. The transition to college: Diverse students, diverse stories. *Research in Higher Education* 37: 1–22.

Tinto, V. 1993. *Leaving college: Rethinking the causes and cures of student attrition.* Chicago, IL: University of Chicago Press.

Tinto, V. 2000. Linking learning and leaving: Exploring the role of the college classroom in student departure. In *Reworking the student departure puzzle,* edited by J.M. Braxton. Vanderbilt University Press.

Umbach, P. D., and M.R. Wawrzynski. 2005. Faculty do matter: The role of college faculty in student learning and engagement. *Research in Higher Education* 46(2): 153–184.

Upcraft, M. L., J.N. Gardner, and B.O. Barefoot. 2005. *Challenging and supporting the first-year student.* San Francisco, CA: Jossey-Bass.

Ward, L., M.J. Siegel, and Z. Davenport. 2012. *First-generation college students: Understanding and improving the experience from recruitment to retention.* San Francisco, CA: Jossey-Bass.

Watson, L. W., Terrell, M. C., and D.J. Wright. 2002. *How minority students experience college.* Sterling, VA: Stylus.

CHAPTER 3

At the Heart of the College Experience

Transforming Groups Into Meaningful Teams by Harnessing the Power of Affiliation-Based Teaching Practices

By Janice A. Fedor and Nicholas D. Young

Introduction

At the heart of the collegiate experience is the quality of the education for students (Wolff and Hughes 2007). For their part, professors are challenged by the twin goals of teaching the material while keeping their students engaged. To this end, instructors must be mindful of the need to make useful, constructive connections between what is taught and the wider world of work (Hargreaves 1997). Being enthusiastic about the subject matter is not nearly enough to survive the demanding prospect of engaging students for an entire semester. Even though instructors may be in love with the subject matter, there is a great chance that the students do not care or that they know very little about it before the class begins.

Students become disengaged from classroom instruction when they fail to see how the material being presented is useful in the real world (Carey 2015; Hargreaves 1997). They also become disengaged when they have no personally relatable context for new information (Carey 2015). Schloss and Cragg (2012) underscore that college and university classrooms cannot be isolated from the reality of the outside environment; attempts to disconnect academia from day-to-day experience leave students wondering why the material matters.

The concept of Affiliation-Based Teaching (ABT) was designed to present material to students by employing a framework that values work experience as well as individual learning styles and needs. According to Wolfe (2010), teaching is more effective when students can tie new learning into what they already know and understand. Professors, then, are encouraged to intentionally motivate students both intrinsically and extrinsically, which requires an appreciation for the individual and his or her learning preferences, life experiences, and future aspirations (Schloss and Cragg 2012).

Why Quick Does Not Work

Dividing students into small groups to work together during class can be an effective instructional method. In K–12 education, the goal is sometimes simply to separate the students who have a considerable amount in common so that they do not end up talking more than working. Having students count off by fours or fives to create groups is quick and easy, but that method can only be relied upon to create groups, not teams. College students should expect more from their group members, and professors should expect more from college-level groups. As a professor, the goal is to turn group work into teamwork, and to do so necessitates an appreciation for the characteristics, potentialities, and stylistic differences between and within learners that can be accomplished without more developmentally appropriate approaches to instruction (Martinez, Smith, and Humphreys 2013). Cohen and Kisker (2009) note that for effective collaboration to occur, students need to be willing to share power, knowledge, and influence. The professor's role is to establish the conditions for such exchanges to occur willingly and productively within a supportive classroom structure. By focusing on practical suggestions that can actually be implemented in the classroom, this chapter will explore the application of Affiliation-Based Teaching principles to address these challenges. While many researchers explore the theory of teaching, far fewer consider the actionable "how-tos" necessary to put those into praxis. While ABT may not be the most effective approach in all classrooms and content areas, it holds considerable promise and value in postsecondary courses where team interaction is employed to maximize student participation and engagement.

Students Profiles—Taking Inventory

Many postsecondary students have worked some type of part-time job, and many have held full-time jobs over summer breaks. Some students even hold full-time jobs while attending college full time. The first step of ABT is to require all students to write their name and list two significant work experiences on an index card. Students who do not have paid work experience are encouraged to write down volunteer experience.

Leadership experience, such as being captain of the swim team or an officer in a club, could also be substituted for paid work experience.

Through this exercise, the instructor learns the names of students and becomes familiar with the type of work experience the students have been previously exposed to before teaching the material in the course. Knowing the students' collective work experience and some individual work experience will help later on in the semester when the instructor wants to give an example or make a comparison between two organizations. Identifying which students can be counted on to stimulate classroom discussion early will help facilitate the rest of the semester.

The ideal time to collect this information is on the first day of class, after the syllabus has been reviewed. A brief explanation of ABT will help empower students and lead in to a discussion of learning styles. Explaining how the brain naturally seeks meaningful patterns by searching through existing networks to find a connection for new information validates the rationale for needing to obtain two prior work experiences (Carey 2015; Wolfe and Hughes 2007). Alternately, the professor may simply express a desire to get to know the students better and start passing out colored index cards. To effectively engage students in the learning process, McEntee (2003) suggests that professors sharpen their skills and employ such practical strategies when approaching their students as fellow adult learners. Otherwise, college students may be quickly turned off to learning and view the professor's approach to be dreadful at worst and not helpful at best (Lattuca and Stark 2009). The goal is for adult learners to feel comfortable with the instructor's approach and to "volunteer" to be active contributors in the classroom (Zepeda 2011).

Learning Styles Assessment

Non-cognitive questionnaires can be administered during class that will reveal to individual students whether they are predominantly visual, auditory, or kinesthetic learners (Celli and Young 2014; Filipczak 1995; Sedlacek 2011). Auxiliary information about learning style study tips can be distributed at this time or posted on online course management systems. Visual learning is the predominant learning style among the general population (70%), followed by auditory learning (20%); at 10%, kinesthetic learners make up the smallest percentage (Celli and Young 2014). A quick show of hands will reveal the unique learning styles breakdown of those students enrolled in a particular course. Although an understanding of individual learning styles is important, it is equally critical for professors to know what to do with this information. Current research suggests that professors have difficulty understanding the meaning of learning style differences and how such differences may be used to improve instructional strategies (Celli and Young 2014).

When seeking to engage students in a conversation about learning style differences, the use of examples is often beneficial. This is the perfect time to discuss the long-term influences of texting, by way of one specific approach. The professor may pose the following question to the class: Why do you think there has been an increase in kinesthetic learners over the last two decades? This question is sure to engage even the most disengaged student, who is probably either texting or thinking about texting. Discuss how the increase in the number of kinesthic learners may be related to the sociocultural influence of cell phones, smartphones, and texting. Kinesthetic learners often feel left out of such conversations, as common teaching strategies are generally directed at visual learners (Celli and Young 2014); thus, this type of example can be especially useful in engaging this group. Kinesthetic learners may then feel empowered to learn that Affiliation-Based Teaching addresses their innate need to learn by doing, moving, and creating (Sedlacek 2011).

Through ABT, students will have the opportunity to use the classroom material by practicing concepts and solving problems that more closely approach real-life situations, which increases information retention by being brain-compatible (Carey 2015; Wolfe 2010). Visual learners should be reminded to take notes on printed out presentation slides that may be posted on the course management system. The visual learners in each group may volunteer to take the notes for the group or create lists and diagrams related to the material.

Auditory learners may feel more optimistic about the course as they learn more effectively by listening to other people talk about the material. The affiliation groups are designed to increase the students' comfort level and aptitude with applying the course material.

Thoughtfully Match the Groups

Most of the time, students' work experience can be grouped into four broad categories: retail/services, coach/camp counselor/teacher, landscaping/physical work, and restaurant/hospitality. A fifth category of service work can be added to encompass a broad array of experiences. Sometimes a specialty category, such as health care, will be necessary because of the number of students enrolled in a course from a specific program. Special groups will appreciate the opportunity to use their area of expertise during class time as the foundation for learning new material, and these groups may even serve as a model for less cohesive teams. The professor's goal is to create four or five groups with roughly the same number of students in each. For that reason, students may be classified using either one of their two listed work experiences, and judgment calls on whether child care belongs under camp counselor or service work are made by the professor. How these groups are formed will depend upon the instructor's goals and the backgrounds of the students enrolled in the course. The overarching point is that groups should be constructed in a way that will bring meaning to the instructional experience and provide each member with opportunities to actively and uniquely contribute to their assigned team.

Non-traditional-age Students

Professors will find that ABT works even more effectively with graduate students, as they are typically older than the traditional college age, and virtually all have significant work experience. Such students might consider this an opportunity to network with other students in their industry sector and exchange business cards during breaks. The overall trend in business is working in groups and teams, so graduate students will acclimate rather quickly to their affiliation group and may even meet outside regular class times (Collins 2013).

Students who regard group work as enjoyable may also improve their own learning by connecting learning to something pleasurable (Willis 2008). Over time, the brain grows more neurons and connects to other neurons, which get more efficient at sending one another signals (Carey 2015; Willis 2008). Consequently, professors who implement ABT methods indirectly help students in all their classes.

Getting Started

Halfway through the second meeting, the affiliation teams should be announced, and students ought to be given the opportunity to change seats and sit together in their assigned four or five groups. This is the time to reiterate why they are in a particular group and allow the students a few minutes to get to know one another. After the groups have had time to meet one another, they can be given the next block of time to complete an in-class assignment based on the material being covered.

Working on an activity immediately after learning new material increases the brain's neuroplasticity, growing and strengthening connections by practicing and using new information (Carey 2015; Willis 2008). Most college-level courses teach concepts, which are declarative memory, and these concepts require elaboration for the brain to create meaning and store them in long-term memory (Carey 2015; Wolfe 2010).

Leveraging Shared Knowledge

The in-class activity should be completed within the context of the group's affiliation. For example, one tool for analysis routinely taught in principles of marketing courses is the situation analysis, or SWOT (Strengths, Weaknesses, Opportunities, and Threats) analysis. Students learning this concept as members of the restaurant/hospitality group will all agree on an organization, for example the Olive Garden, and then complete the in-class analysis. Even if only one member of the group actually worked at the Olive Garden, the other group members have restaurant or hospitality experience that makes them sufficiently familiar with the industry. Being knowledgeable in an industry and knowing the industry vernacular allows for the possibility of more in-depth analysis. Other restaurants will have had similar challenges, and the students can use their shared work backgrounds as a basis for analysis.

Ideally, assignments should focus on relating the material to enduring concepts that generalize from one era to the next and information that can be used throughout a student's life (Wolfe 2010). Creativity tools, such as the SCAMPER (Collins 2013), can be learned and practiced within the context of affiliation groups but then utilized in other courses. This technique should increase the level of engagement as students begin discussing how they might use a particular tool or knowledge.

Elaborating on new material in this manner creates meaning and increases memory of the material (Carey 2015; Willis 2008; Wolfe 2010). Students may struggle with discussing proprietary information about their places of employment, especially when analyzing weaknesses of a present employer, with other group members. They can be reminded to use hypothetical scenarios if they fear divulging trade secrets.

Writing for Wikis

Affiliation-Based Teaching gives students enrolled in writing courses a more effective forum for peer editing and review of each other's work. Students who share similar professional backgrounds are able to offer feedback that is more applicable to the topic. Learning how to collaborate with others who share similar knowledge may help students develop a skill needed to contribute to wikis. Contributing to wikis, which may be expected in contemporary positions, is considered a different type of writing (Bovee and Thill 2012; Shwom and Snyder 2012). Consumer marketing content in the form of conversations, blogs, and websites is also becoming more important than ever (Bovee and Thill 2012). Content marketing is increasingly essential for organizations and has become a premier communication tool for entrepreneurs (Bovee and Thill 2012).

Affinity for Affiliation: "Are We Doing Our Groups Today?"

Students may become fond of their group and of their group's work and time spent together, possibly asking the professor if the group time is going to happen during a particular class period or not. This factor may increase the overall attendance rate for the course as well as general positive feelings toward the course, which may be reflected in course evaluations.

Some unexpected outcomes of ABT include an increase in students' self-efficacy. Students who were too shy to speak up during the previous semester may assume a leadership position within a group of students with whom they feel comfortable. Members within affiliation groups speak with confidence about their own ideas using management and marketing terminology because they are familiar with these concepts within their own framework of real-world experience.

Seamlessly Bridge Class Meetings

Sometimes the class is right in the middle of a heated discussion, but students begin packing up because the class period is ending. Utilizing ABT can help the professor pick up these discussions almost right where the previous class left off by recreating the scene, the players, and the topic. Group leaders can be made responsible for keeping track of notes and taking pictures of the whiteboard so that collective notes can be restored.

Another benefit of ABT is the guidance it provides the professor in connecting one class to the next, which can be especially helpful when the professor runs out of time during a class period and must resume the lesson on a different day. Students have an easier time remembering what project they were working on and the theme of the general discussion of the group rather than what the instructor was lecturing about during the previous class session (Hurt 2012). Reviewing what each affiliation group was working on during the last class meeting can be an effective way to review material while aiding long-term memory retention (Wolfe 2010).

Increasing Academic Rigor through Enhanced Analysis

Utilizing ABT also provides an opportunity for the professor and students to compare models and tools across different sectors or settings. For example, in business, market segmentation and product life cycle analysis are different depending on the tangibility of the product or service. Group activities conducted within affiliation groups allow the opportunity to discuss the nuances of different sectors, increasing the students' understanding and retention of the material (Jensen 2008). Rotating the group speaker or representative at each class gives all of the students the chance to develop their speaking skills.

Blocks of Time

Keeping students engaged for longer class periods, such as 75 minutes, can be especially challenging for new professors. Incorporating ABT into long sessions is an ideal way to texture the instruction and accommodate kinesthetic learners. Holding class for an hour and 15 minutes allows the instructor time to introduce new material for the first 25 minutes, then direct the affiliation groups to work for the next 25 minutes on an assigned activity that reinforces the material within their framework of existing knowledge (Carey 2015; Hurt 2012; Willis 2008). The last 25 minutes of the class period can be spent comparing the applications of the new material across the different student groups.

Friendly Competition Increases Motivation

Many students, especially athletes, love to compete and will try harder to outperform others' work when it is publicly displayed on a whiteboard. Friendly competition between groups can help motivate students to learn material when the groups are competing against one another. Classrooms with stadium-style seats bolted to the ground may present a physical limitation, but students are generally able to work through these and other difficulties when they are motivated by competition.

Group Size Matters

Affiliation groups work well with about five or six students assigned to each group, an ideal size for maximum productivity (Williams 2010). A group larger than six students will not be conducive to every student having an opportunity to contribute his or her thoughts, which decreases individual and overall group learning (Hurt 2012). If appropriate and if the numbers are relatively even, some courses may employ a semester-long "Battle of the Sexes" where teams are gender-based and compete weekly for points.

Extra Benefits of Affiliation-Based Teaching

Students will typically begin to share notes on the group activities and course material, and some may voluntarily study together. Sometimes groups will share examples with other groups so that students can be exposed to more detailed analyses of different industry sectors.

ABT gives students a framework upon which to learn new material and a small learning group within the larger classroom community. ABT promotes long-term retention of knowledge by working with the brain's natural process; rehearsing newly learned material stimulates dendrites (Carey 2015). Growing more dendrites connects new information into neural networks, which solidifies the knowledge (Carey 2015; Willis 2008). Also, having the students work collaboratively on a group problem and then present their findings during class facilitates learning for all learning styles.

Conclusion

McEntee (2003) found that student engagement is critical to academic achievement and success at all educational levels. In addition, relational learning, group interaction, and real-world connections are necessary components of high-quality adult education (Hagenauer and Volet 2014). Professors must continually balance the requirement to meet the developmental needs and expectations of their college and university students—the adults who inhabit their classrooms—while seeking to teach the assigned subject matter essential to promoting critical thinking, an informed citizenry, and future career preparations. For those undergraduate and graduate courses where student interaction and active engagement is desired, Affiliation-Based Teaching techniques have been found to be particularly useful in addressing individual learning style differences and relational needs. ABT relies on the use of student groups formed around unique student experiences and strengths with the goal of promoting higher levels of knowledge acquisition, retention, and educational engagement. ABT works well with a variety of courses. Keeping track of group assignments will generate greater creativity and clarification on the part of the professor the following semester, which will improve the effectiveness of the activity and the overall learning outcomes of the course. The time it takes a professor to collect student information on index cards and create affiliation groups is a rather small investment that holds the promise of being educationally meaningful for those who matter most: the students.

Points to Remember

- Connecting classroom instruction with the learning styles and real-world experiences and aspirations of the individual students is essential. Styles and differences are identified and viewed as individual strengths to be brought to the team format.
- Affiliation-Based Teaching (ABT) practices organize classroom instruction around meaningful student groups formed on the basis of student experience, interests, or other selected criteria that promote student engagement.
- ABT begins with a self-inventory process in which student learning styles and differences are identified and viewed as individual strengths to be brought to the team format.

- The ABT approach has been found to promote knowledge sharing, increase social connection with like-minded students, and make classroom instruction in certain subjects and long-block periods especially meaningful for students.
- In courses that seek to promote student interaction, ABT generally encourages higher levels of knowledge acquisition, memory retention, and overall student engagement.

References

Bovee, C. L., and J.V. Thill. 2012. *Business communication today*. 11th ed. Boston: MA, Pearson.

Carey, K. 2015. *The end of college: Creating the future of learning and the university of everywhere*. New York, NY: Penguin.

Celli, L., and N. Young. 2014. *Learning style perspectives: Impact in the classroom*. 3rd ed. Madison, WI: Atwood Publishing.

Cohen, A., and C. Kisker. 2009. *The shaping of American higher education: Emergency and growth of the contemporary system*. San Francisco, CA: Jossey-Bass.

Collins, K. 2013. *Exploring business version 2.0*. Washington, DC: Flat World Knowledge.

Filipczak, B. 1995. Different strokes: Learning styles in the classroom. *Training, 32*(3), 43.

Hagenauer, G. and S.E. Volet. 2014. Teacher-student relationship at university: An important yet under-researched field. Retrieved from http://www.tandfonline.com/doi/full/10.1080/03054985.2014.921613?scroll=topandneedAccess=true

Hargreaves, A. 1997. *Rethinking educational change with heart and mind*. Alexandria, VA: ASCD Yearbook.

Hurt, J. 2012, January 31. 10 brain-based learning laws that trump traditional education. *Velvet Chainsaw Consulting*. Retrieved from http://velvetchainsaw.com/2012/01/31/10-brainbased-learning-laws-that-trump-traditional-education/

Jensen, E. 2008. *Brain-based learning: The new paradigm of teaching and learning*. 2nd ed. Thousand Oaks, CA: Corwin.

Lattucca, L., and J. Stark. 2009. *Shaping the college curriculum: Academic plans in context*. San Francisco: Jossey-Bass.

Martinez, M., B. Smith, and K. Humphreys. 2013. *Creating a service culture in higher education*. Sterling, VA: Stylus.

McEntee, G. H. 2003. *At the heart of teaching: A guide to reflective practice*. New York: Teachers College Press.

Schloss, P., and K.M. Cragg. 2012. *Organization and administration in higher education*. New York: Routledge.

Sedlacek, W. E. 2011. Using noncognitive variables in assessing readiness for higher education. *Readings on Equal Education* 25:187-205.

Shwom, B., and L.G. Snyder. 2012. *Business communication: Polishing your professional presence.* Boston: Prentice Hall.

Williams, C. 2010. *Management.* 2nd ed. Mason, OH: South-Western Cengage.

Willis, J. 2008. *Teaching the brain to read: Strategies for improving fluency, vocabulary, and comprehension.* Alexandria, VA: ASCD.

Wolfe, P. 2010. *Brain matters: Translating research into classroom practice.* Alexandria, VA: ASCD.

Wolf, P., and J.C. Hughes. 2007. *Curriculum development in higher education: Faculty-driven processes and practices.* Hoboken, NJ: Wiley and Sons.

Zapeda, S. J. 2011. *Professional development: What works.* New York: Routledge.

CHAPTER 4

The Professor's Role in Teaching Subject-Specific Scholarly Writing

By Nadine Bonda

Introduction

Professors are teaching a more diverse population of students——in terms of ethnicity, income, and preparation—than ever before, and they are being called upon to teach in ways that develop both critical and creative thinking (Hainlaine, Gaines, Long Feather, Padilla, and Terry 2010). In addition, professors are often required to teach basic writing skills as well as scholarly writing. Over 25% of high school graduates in 2012 did not meet American College Testing (ACT) entrance exam benchmarks for all four main subjects, and 60% of these graduates did not meet the ACT benchmarks in at least two of the four subjects (Sheehy 2012). According to Balfanz (2009), student writing in high school is often not a priority, with only 8% of high school seniors reporting that they were asked to do the equivalent of college writing both in terms of the number of papers they were assigned to write and in the length of those papers.

According to a survey of 2,462 educators by the Pew Research Center (Purcell, Heaps, Buchanan, and Friedrich 2013), educators were concerned that there was an immediate need to teach students about how and why to write for different audiences as a result of social media. Survey participants identified a need to address widespread student use of abbreviations or truncated forms of expression, which may interfere with students' abilities to write more complex papers and to demonstrate their ability to think critically about complicated topics and issues (Purcell et al. 2013). Another need the educators cited was to teach students the distinctions between formal and informal writing and the audiences for these different types of writing (Purcell et al. 2013). Thus, it is necessary for professors to be adept at actively teaching postsecondary scholars the importance of academic writing and how it is accomplished.

Academic Writing and Critical Thinking

Academic writing, as defined by Bair and Mader (2013), is writing for a specific and informed reader that uses reason to make an argument or take a position and is often grounded in both scholarly literature and primary sources. This approach to writing needs to be learned, and there is often a progression to learning the art of scholarly writing that students need to proceed through.

According to Ballard and Clanchy (1997), students move through several stages in their journey toward becoming fluent scholarly writers. They often start with the ability to summarize and describe information; then move on to the ability to question, judge, and recombine information; and finally acquire the ability to recognize the need to search for additional ideas and data sources and use these ideas/sources to develop new explanations of the phenomenon being studied. By the third stage, students should be able to summarize, question, synthesize, and move toward the creation of new knowledge, new interpretations of previous knowledge, and new forms of evidence to support the findings (Ballard and Clanchy 1997).

Inherent in the development of strong academic writing skills is the ability to think critically. Bean describes academic writing as the "exterior sign of an interior thinking process" (2001, 20), and he emphasizes the necessity to teach thesis-based analytical and argumentative writing as well as the essential academic inquiry process that leads to deep thinking and strong academic writing. Goldberger links thinking and writing by stating that "writing is thinking made manifest" (2014, 1), clearly suggesting that clear thinking is essential to produce clear writing. Although Elder and Paul (2006) make the connection between the ability to write well and the ability to think well, one does not necessarily guarantee the other.

Harris (2006) notes that when students are not good writers, it may conceal their critical thinking ability. As students begin the process of scholarly writing, many have not actively thought about how research articles are constructed. They also may not have examined scholarly writing closely enough to understand how its construction is different from the construction of other types of writing, nor have they perhaps even envisioned that academic writing is a specific form of writing. This lack of familiarity with the genre can be problematic and calls for a focused approach to teaching academic writing.

Disciplinary Discourse

To complicate the issue, research indicates that scholarly writing requirements differ among disciplines, so the kind of writing that is expected in one discipline is not necessarily what is expected in another (Leki 2007). The term *discourse community* was coined in the 1980s to describe how the beliefs and values of a specific community can influence the way people within that group communicate orally and in writing (Hyon 1996). Every academic subject could certainly be considered a unique discourse community.

Methods and forms of writing can differ markedly from department to department across the postsecondary institutional landscape. Although writing expectations differ among disciplines and can be community specific, the larger goal is for scholars to use their critical thinking and analytical skills as well as their reasoning and persuasion skills while demonstrating a deep understanding of the subject matter and their ability to shape and defend an argument (Hyland 2013). According to Dahme, Kononova, and Tolchinsky, academic writing has four major functions: "communicative, epistemic, dialogic, and constructive of social identity and social integrations" (2013, 943). Because these functions are subject specific, students need to be familiar with and able to converse in the specialized language of their particular discipline.

Inducting Students into Community Discourse

Because each discipline or academic community has different norms by which it judges scholarly writing, it is important that each professor sees it as his or her role to facilitate students' induction into the particular discipline's writing style. This does not eliminate the need for a general writing course, as appropriate sentence structure, paragraph composition, and grammatical construction are necessary prerequisites for strong scholarly writing. However, it is the professoriate's role to familiarize students in their particular discipline with the norms, expectations, and writing conventions of that specific community (Hyland 2013).

Currie (1993) argues that professors must use purposeful writing assignments to initiate their students into a discipline's particular style of thinking. If writing assignments are carefully developed and sequenced, students can gradually be introduced to the norms for writing in a particular discipline. Different academic disciplines will require different kinds of writing assignments by which scholars are evaluated. For example, writing in history is different from writing in the sciences; a research paper using quantitative methods will look significantly different from a research paper using qualitative methods. In addition, students in some disciplines may do less writing than students in other disciplines (Leki 2007). Consequently, students may have different scholarly writing needs depending on the type of writing they will be expected to do, the amount of writing that will be required, and the context of the writing within their particular areas of study (Johns 1997).

In a study of 20 university professors by Hyland (2013), the following abilities were identified as their highest priorities in the academic writing they sought from their students: expressing themselves and engaging with a discourse in the past; addressing a research question in a structured, thoughtful manner with evidence and logical conclusions; demonstrating the use of the scientific method; thinking logically; learning and grasping new content; and writing a persuasive argument with supportive evidence. This same study found that students often receive feedback that is "prescriptive, cursory, and largely focused on content, thus conveying the idea that writing conventions are absolute, generic, and obvious" (Hyland 2013, 251). Hyland (2013) concludes by asserting that feedback, if given differently, could help develop students' writing skills and encourage them to revise their work.

The purpose and benefits of scholarly writing do not differ among disciplines. Levessaur (2014) provides a straightforward list of these benefits. First, academic writing incorporates the upper levels of Bloom's taxonomy that address higher-order thinking: analysis and synthesis. Students should consider how they will analyze their findings and synthesize them into a theory, a new body of knowledge, or a branch of knowledge that supports the findings of others. Second, learners need to demonstrate that they can read and analyze the writings of other authors, synthesize the writing, and combine it with others' thoughts to make a sound argument. It is this synthesis that will build the foundation for each student's own work. Third, Levessaur (2014) calls for the writing to be objective; it must present both sides of the argument as presented in the literature without the students' own opinions. Fourth, Levessaur (2014) concludes by adding that the passive voice and the first- or second-person should not be used in scholarly writing, which focuses students on writing more formally, maturely, purposefully, precisely, and conscientiously than they ordinarily would. Through careful feedback, postsecondary students should be able to develop in each of these four areas.

The induction of the student into the particular discipline is an important role for the professor. Johns (1997) writes that to produce a strong scholarly piece of writing in a particular discipline, the student must have an understanding of the culture, circumstances, purposes, and motives of the discipline. Prior (1998) adds that learning to write in some disciplines involves negotiations between students and others in the discipline, including professors, peers, and mentors. This knowledge is often not obvious and the student can be well served by a mentor who helps to demystify these factors for him or her.

Thinking Like a Scholar

Richardson (2000) describes novice writers as those using a static writing model: they conduct research, write up what they did, and report the findings. The shift to scholarly writing can be daunting. A new and different kind of thinking is expected—thinking that has more depth, synthesizes the ideas of others, and uses that synthesis to argue an opinion or create new knowledge. As students transition from high school to college, "they frequently become immersed in jargon, fragmented ideas, unsupported opinions, and a disorganization 'fog' " (Harris 2006, 136). Helping students emerge from that "fog" is key to promoting their success in becoming strong scholarly writers.

Regardless of their writing skills, not all college and university students are good thinkers. Toor (2010) recalls George Orwell's essay *Politics and the English Language,* in which Orwell argues the connections between bad thinking and bad writing. Good thinking skills can be taught, and students—at both the undergraduate and graduate levels alike—may need to be taught to think like scholars before they can attempt to write like scholars. Caffarella and Barnett (2000) note that even doctoral students often do not think like scholars. As Ronald states, "composition theorists continue to describe writing as a way of 'knowing' " (1987, 23). Clear thinking is a pathway to cogent scholarly writing.

The Importance of Feedback

Feedback can be a powerful influence on the development of student thinking and student writing. In his inaugural lecture as Professor of Education at the University of Auckland, Hattie reported that as a result of his work with over 500 meta-analyses of the factors that influence learning, "the most powerful single moderator that enhances achievement is feedback. The simplest prescription for improving education must be 'dollops of feedback' " (1999, 9).

For feedback to be effective, it needs to be specific to a particular learning context. Feedback must answer these three questions: What are the goals? What progress is made toward those goals? What activities can be undertaken to make additional progress? (Hattie and Timperley 2007). Helpful feedback can restructure understandings, confirm whether certain understandings are correct or incorrect, delineate gaps in the research, point the student in a helpful direction, or provide alternative strategies for the student to consider. Essentially, feedback needs to fill the gap between what the student already knows and what the student needs to understand for the writing and the thinking behind it to be most effective (Sadler 1998).

According to Hyland (2013), feedback should play a role in the cognitive development of students by helping them better understand their own strengths and weaknesses while assisting them in acquiring greater knowledge of discipline-specific subject matter and developing their writing skills with the conventions particular to their discipline. Hyland (2013) adds that feedback can help students learn how to state a claim, evaluate ideas, make connections, think about why they are doing their research, solve the problems they encounter, and develop a framework for their writing. Hyland (2013) contends that the overall goal of feedback is to help students develop a conceptual understanding of the discipline.

Feedback should examine a particular aspect of a student's work and provide specific knowledge or ask specific questions of the student to help guide the student's thinking. Feedback is more effective when it addresses the process that underlies the task; feedback is less effective when it is given in the form of praise, rewards, or punishment. Not surprisingly, feedback is most effective when the student does not feel that his or her self-esteem is being threatened (Hattie and Timperley 2007).

Caffarella and Barnett (2000) found that writing had to be an iterative process and that scholarly writing improved more quickly and became stronger when students continuously received feedback from both their professors and their peers. Consequently, they make a solid argument for building ongoing feedback and peer editing into the fabric of every course. Goldberger (2014) goes even further by arguing that writing needs to be embedded in every subject and cannot be delegated only to those professors who specifically teach writing courses.

Piercy, Sprenkle, and McDaniel (1996) point out that graduate students are often adult learners, and adult learners need to be engaged and challenged while also being supported. This support needs to come in the form of constructive and objective feedback as well as clear expectations for what comprises scholarly writing.

The Potential of Instructional Rubrics

Rubrics have become a mainstay in many classrooms. Carnegie Mellon University's Eberly Center for Teaching Excellence and Educational Innovation (2015) defines a rubric as a scoring tool that lays out the expectations for an assignment or a work product. The rubric breaks the assignment down into its components and clearly delineates the level of work at various stages of mastery. Andrade (2000) expands this definition to describe what she calls "the instructional rubric." Instructional rubrics will support student learning while helping the student develop sophisticated thinking skills. When used correctly, rubrics not only aid in evaluation and accountability, but they also have an important instructional role (Andrade 2000). All rubrics, including instructional rubrics, feature a list of criteria highlighting the key elements of an assignment as well as quality levels. However, instructional rubrics also provide informative feedback to students about their works in progress and offer a more detailed evaluative description of their final products. According to Andrade (2000), instructional rubrics serve several purposes: they clarify teacher expectations, provide students with detailed feedback about their strengths and areas of improvement, enhance student learning, support skill development and development of understanding, and promote clear thinking.

Writing skills can be an important element of an instructional rubric and a part of any assignment. Saddler and Andrade write, "An important goal in writing instruction is to help students develop the self-regulation skills needed to successfully manage the intricacies of the writing process. Instructional rubrics can provide the scaffolding that students need to become self-regulated writers" (2004, 48). For example, Saddler (2003) describes how rubrics can be used in the editing process by laying out the components of the edit and describing levels of quality from poor to excellent in spelling, punctuation, and grammar. Professors can help students become reflective critics of their own work and promote self-regulation through the use of instructional rubrics that include a writing component (Saddler and Andrade 2004).

The Power of Peer Feedback

In their study of 42 graduate students over five years, Caffarella and Barnett (2000) found that ongoing feedback from both professors and peers was integral to developing confidence as well as skill as academic writers. Their findings point to the importance of peer feedback and how students reported that peer critiquing; that is, both critiquing others writing and getting feedback on their own writing from peers was essential to their development as good writers.

When students were asked to critique others' writing and receive critiques from their peers, they admitted experiencing initial feelings of insecurity about whether they could provide useful feedback, as well as anxiety about the kind of feedback they might receive (Caffarella and Barnett 2000). Lamott (1994) confirmed that although writing independently can be less stressful, receiving feedback from others, particularly peers, is important in the development of ideas and writing. However, after the students went through the peer review process, they experienced far less of an emotional reaction to feedback and a deeper appreciation for being able to compare others' writing to their own as well as to learn about others' academic areas of interest (Caffarella and Barnett 2000). Supportive peer relationships, such as those that could develop from meaningful group interaction and peer editing, could help individual students further develop their thinking skills (Cranton 1994).

Unless students are given concrete guidelines and specific questions to answer, the task of reviewing a peer's work can become emotionally charged, and students will respond by giving rather neutral, generic evaluations, such as "I liked your paper," which provide no real substance or guidance as to how the student can improve his or her writing (Nilson 2003). In an online strategy for helping teachers improve student writing, The Teaching Center at Washington University (n.d.) comments that if students understand and are fully engaged in the peer review process, they should have a clear idea of the criteria they must use when writing a paper and when commenting on a paper. "They should also start to see themselves as writers and readers who have a stake in learning to recognize and to produce effective writing—as peers who learn more when they learn to communicate more effectively with one another" (Teaching Center, n.d., n.p.)

The Emotions Associated with Learning Academic Writing

Scholarly writing can be an emotional experience for the student. Because academic writing is rarely explicitly taught, students may experience a high level of fear and anxiety, which has the potential to cripple their early writing attempts (Cameron, Nairn, and Higgins 2009). When novice writers see only finished, perfectly polished work in journals and other texts, they do not always recognize that writing can be a messy process that requires several rewrites.

Cameron et al.'s (2009) study followed 12 graduate students through a writing workshop. Students beginning to learn the writing process expressed feelings of self-doubt and insecurity, intimidation about starting to write, uncertainty regarding where to get ideas, and concern about the worth and relevance of current ideas (Cameron et al. 2009). In addition, students noted the following concerns: a struggle to find relevant research, a deficit in skills and confidence, and a genuine fear of being critiqued or judged in relation to other authors or of not meeting the expectations that others have for them (Cameron et al. 2009).

At the end of the writing workshop, students acknowledged a camaraderie with peers in their mutual struggles with learning to write and their shared feelings of self-doubt; they all agreed that writing could be slow and painful at times (Cameron et al. 2009). Overall, though, students viewed themselves as better, stronger writers after having learned how to approach the task of scholarly writing. When asked about what they learned of significance in this academic writing workshop, students gave rather practical responses, reporting that beginning with a draft is important and that the draft should then lead to several rewrites, as more rewrites will only improve the quality of the writing (Cameron et al. 2009).

Cameron et al. (2009) offer two pieces of advice for professors who wish to help their students hone their skills in the craft of scholarly writing. First, the professor must not ignore the emotional side of writing, acknowledging that even the most experienced writers can feel self-doubt and anxiety. Second, on a regular basis, novice writers must share their work with others. Getting feedback early on, with each draft, exposes the student to constructive criticism and helpful suggestions, thereby reducing the learner's fear of "being exposed for lack of ability," so to speak, by getting this worry out of the way near the start of a writing assignment. Early and continued feedback throughout the writing process will help beginning writers move from seeing themselves as inexperienced academic writers to skilled writers with legitimate voices who are capable of making contributions to the field.

Conclusion

Academic writing is drastically different from the writing that most students produce on a regular basis (Purcell et al. 2013). Further, academic writing varies considerably from discipline to discipline across the postsecondary institutional landscape (Leki 2007). Each academic discipline has a set of norms and writing conventions, often known but not written, that define the discourse in that discipline. Scholarly writing can produce significant anxiety for college and university students primarily because they are being asked to write in a way that is rarely explicitly taught (Cameron et al. 2009). It is, therefore, incumbent upon professors to clearly delineate the writing conventions of their particular discipline and induct students into the discipline so that these learners become able to engage with others in the discipline and to share research (Leki 2007).

An important part of the process of developing strong academic writers within a given discipline is the provision of feedback that helps students create a framework for their writing, restructure their ideas, consider alternative strategies, and present their ideas in a format that is recognized within the discipline. Most useful is targeted feedback focused on the product or the process used to create the product (Cameron et al. 2009). Using these techniques, professors will actively and successfully guide their students into the world of scholarly writing.

Points to Remember

- The role of the professoriate is changing as the student population becomes more diverse and as the need increases for building learners' skills in three key areas: critical thinking, basic writing, and subject-specific scholarly writing.
- Inherent in the development of strong academic writing ability is the ability to think critically.
- Research indicates that scholarly writing requirements differ across various academic disciplines, and the kind of writing that is expected in one discipline is not necessarily what is expected in another.

- Students need to be familiar with and able to converse in the specialized language of their particular discipline, and it is the professor's role to introduce students to the particular concepts and terminology of a given discipline.
- If writing assignments are carefully developed and sequenced, students can gradually be inducted into the norms for writing in a particular discipline.
- Good thinking skills can be taught, and students may need to be taught to think like scholars before they can attempt to write like scholars.

References

Andrade, H. 2000. Using rubrics to promote thinking and learning. *Educational Leadership* 55(5):13–18.

Bair, M. A., and C.E. Mader. 2013. Academic writing at the graduate level: Improving the curriculum through faculty collaboration. *Journal of University Teaching and Learning Practice* 10(1). Retrieved from http://ro.uow.edu.au/jutlp/vol10/iss1/4/

Balfanz, R. 2009. Can the American high school become an avenue of advancement for all? *The Future of Children* 19(1):17–36.

Ballard, B., and J. Clanchy. 1997. *Teaching international students: A brief guide for lecturers and supervisors.* Deakin, ACT: IDP Education Australia.

Bean, J. C. 1996. *Engaging ideas: The professor's guide to integrating writing, critical thinking, and active learning in the classroom.* San Francisco CA: Jossey-Bass.

Cameron, J., K. Nairn, and J. Higgins. 2009, May. Demystifying academic writing: Reflections on emotions. *Journal of Geography in Higer Educaiton* 33(2):269-284.

Caffarella, R. S., and B.G. Barnett. 2000. Teaching doctoral students to become scholarly writers. *Studies in Higher Educaiton* 25(1):39-52.

Carnegie Mellon University. 2015. *Grading and performance rubrics.* Pittsburg, PA: Eberly.

Center for Teaching Excellence and Educaitonal Innovation, Carnegie Mello University. Retrieved from https://www.cmu.edu/teaching/designteach/teach/rubrics.html

Cranton, P. 1994. *Understanding and practicing transformative learning: A guide for educators of adults.* San FranciscoCA: Jossey-Bass.

Currie, P. 1993. Entering a disciplinary community: Conceptual activities required to write for one introductory university course. *Journal of Second Language Writing* 2(2): 101–117.

Dahme, A. P., V.A. Kononova, and L. Tolchinsky. 2013. Triptych approach: Cognitive, social, and linguistic perspectives for analyzing academic writing. *Journal of Siberian Federal University Humanities and Social Sciences* 7(6):943–956. Retrieved from http://www.researchgate.net/publication/264598797_Triptych_Approach_Cognitive_Social_and_Linguistic_Perspectives_for_Analyzing_Academic_Writing

Elder, L., and R. Paul. 2006. Critical thinking and the art of substantive writing: Part II. *Journal of Developmental Education* 29(3):38–39.

Goldberger, E. 2014, April 24. Everyone should teach writing. *Inside Higher Ed.* Retrieved from http://www.insidehighered.com/views/2014/04/24/essay-why-all-faculty-need-consider-teaching-writing-their-responsibility#sthash.4Keu6d6C.dpbs

Hainlaine, L., M. Gaines, C. Long Feather, E. Padilla, and E. Terry. 2010. Changing students, faculty, and institutions in the twenty-first century. *Peer Review* 12(3):1–8.

Harris, M. J. 2006. Three steps to teaching abstract and critique writing. *International Journal of Teaching and Learning in Higher Education* 17(2):136–146.

Hattie, J. A. 1999, August 2. *Influences on student learning* (Inaugural Lecture, University of Auckland, New Zealand). Retrieved from https://cdn.auckland.ac.nz/assets/education/hattie/docs/influences-on-student-learning.pdf

Hattie, J. A., and H. Timperley. 2007. The power of feedback. *Review of Educational Research* 77(1):81-112.

Hyland, K. 2013. Faculty feedback: Perceptions and practices in L2 disciplinary writing. *Journal of Second Language Writing* 22(3):240–253.

Hyon, S. 1996. Genre in three traditions: Implications for ESL. *TESOL Quarterly* 30: 693–720.

Johns, A. M. 1997. *Text, role, and context: Developing academic literacies.* New York: Cambridge Academic Press.

Lamott, A. 1994. *Bird by bird: Some instructions on writing and life.* New York: Doubleday.

Leki, I. 2007. *Undergraduates in a second language: Challenges and complexities of academic literacy development.* New York, NY: Earlbaum.

Levessaur, R. 2014. *Scholarly writing.* Retrieved from http://www.mindfirepress.com/Scholarly_Writing.html

Nilson, L. 2003. Improving student peer feedback. *College Teaching* 51(1):34–38.

Piercy, F. P., D.H. Sprenkle, and S.H. McDaniel. 1996. Teaching professional writing to family therapists: Three approaches. *Journal of Marital and Family Therapy* 22:163–179.

Prior, P. 1998. *Writing/disciplinarily: A sociohistoric account of literate activity in the academy.* New York NY: Routledge.

Purcell, K., A. Heaps, J. Buchanan, and L. Friedrich. 2013, February 28. *How teachers are using technology at home and in their classrooms.* Washington, DC: Pew Research Center's Internet and American Life Project. Retrieved from http://www.pewinternet.org/2013/02/28/how-teachers-are-using-technology-at-home-and-in-their-classrooms/

Richardson, L. 2000. Writing: A method of inquiry. In *Handbook of qualitative research* 2nd ed. Edited by N. K. Denzin and Y. S. Lincoln. Thousand Oaks, CA: SAGE.

Ronald, K. 1987. The politics of teaching professional writing. *Journal of Advanced Composition* 7(1–2): 23–30.

Saddler, B,. and H. Andrade. 2004. The writing rubric. *Educational Leadership* 62(2):48–52.

Sadler, D. R. 1998. Formative assessment: Revisiting the territory. *Assessment in Education: Principles, Policy, and Practice* 5:77–84.

Sheehy, K. 2012, August 22. High school students not prepared for college career. *U.S. News and World Report*. Retrieved from http://www.usnews.com/education/blogs/high-school-notes/2012/08/22/high-school-students-not-prepared-for-college-career

Teaching Center at Washington University in St. Louis. N.d.. *Using peer review to help student improve writing*. Retrieved from https://teachingcenter.wustl.edu/resources/writing-assignments-feedback/using-peer-review-to-help-students-improve-their-writing/

Toor, R. 2010, April 15. Bad writing and bad thinking. *The Chronicle of Higher Education*. Retrieved fromhttp://chronicle.com/article/Bad-WritingBad-Thinking/65031/

CHAPTER 5

Leadership in the Professoriate
Components Necessary for Growth

By Lynne M. Celli

Introduction

The importance of leadership in the professoriate has increased dramatically in contemporary higher education. To this end, postsecondary institutions recognize that for faculty to assume leadership roles in individual departments or advance into administrative positions, many components need to be successfully implemented. The following are among the variables that rise to the top of a long list of critical components that promote leadership in the professoriate: expanding the role of the professoriate, supporting professional development, reviewing and modifying the processes and procedures related to hiring and promotion, and emphasizing quality teaching and leadership in higher education. These variables must all be interwoven for high-quality leadership in the professoriate to manifest itself (Hill 2012).

The Role of Leadership in the Professoriate

Scholarship has long been the primary focus of the professoriate (Hill 2012). However, the definition of scholarship continues to evolve and expand in higher education today. Scholarship now includes the integration and application of content instead of just the mastery of content; the teaching and learning processes now center more on making connections to real-life applications for both students and professors (Hill 2012). Simply stated, faculty members have the desire to assume redefined leadership roles (Barden and Curry 2013). Historically, there have been obstacles to reaching this new view of the professoriate. Leadership roles, such as department chairs, have been temporary and rotating. This organizational structure lends itself to frequently shifting visions and missions within any given department as the leader changes.

The one constant is the mission and vision of the institution (Barden and Curry 2013). Although this is important, leadership that encourages goal setting, development, the expansion of members' skill levels, and evolution in the application of current research becomes problematic as the leadership in the department rotates. In addition, financial constraints and limited professional development budgets to promote leadership among faculty certainly complicate the matter even further. The historical mindset has been that faculty often become suspicious of colleagues who remain in administrative roles for too long (Barden and Curry 2013). Antiquated decision-making structures have limited processes for tapping into the leadership skills of professors. Many colleges and universities do have faculty committees; however, the translation of recommendations from these committees to the overarching changes that occur on campus is sometimes barely recognizable. Faculty who have the desire to offer their leadership skills at the highest possible level of the organization may not even be considered in the institution's leadership structure. This further disenfranchises professors who sincerely want to lead at their colleges or universities (Barden and Curry 2013). Faculty as leaders, then, must be viewed as a constituency that will continue to move the institution forward, not as a threat that will have negative consequences. Placing a new perspective on the contemporary role of the professoriate is necessary; senior administrators in colleges and universities must begin to view faculty as leaders by developing varied systems that encourage this paradigm shift. This evolution includes reshaping the view of faculty in the areas of ongoing, bidirectional dialogue and organic decision-making processes. Further, collegiality and autonomy should not be viewed as mutually exclusive but as interfacing regularly (Barden and Curry 2013). Shifting the paradigm in these ways will not only encourage a change in the overall view of the professoriate, but it will also create a change in the mindset of faculty as leaders.

What Leadership in the Professoriate Looks Like

What do the many facets of current leadership in the professoriate look like in practical terms? Typically, the professoriate is described as being a scholarly role centered on academic research and writing for publication in peer-reviewed journals, exemplary teaching at the postsecondary level, and service at the institution of higher education as well as beyond the college or university. This service could include membership on a state, regional, or national committee or board; being elected to chair a national or international conference; or planning a local, state, or regional event (Hill 2012). Also included in the service component of the professoriate is service within the college or university itself. This service includes being chair of an internal committee, writing and obtaining grants for the college or university to further its mission and vision, participating substantively in faculty meetings concerning the goals of the organization, and volunteering for activities that are beyond the academic scope of the institution (Hill 2012). As stated earlier, these service-related responsibilities are specific to the professoriate. However, upon closer scrutiny, many of these duties also may be categorized as leadership functions in the professoriate.

Chairing a national or international conference and planning a local, state, or regional conference are examples of leadership in the professoriate at its best. In these concrete service roles, professors represent their personal colleges or universities beyond their campuses, making an impact at expanded levels. This impact may then transcend other campuses. Making a positive influence in higher education beyond one's own campus demonstrates leadership skills in the professoriate. Thus, when truly understanding what the overarching responsibilities of the professoriate are, it is clear that expanding these implied responsibilities puts the professor on the pathway to leadership.

Leaders in college and university settings possess positive characteristics, including an awareness of their own leadership strengths and weaknesses. Faculty who lead in the professoriate know the culture of the organization; maintain high standards of values; are aware of the needs of their colleagues; and are passionate about teaching, service, and leading (Boyatzis and McKee 2005). Faculty members committed to leadership build trust among their colleagues, understand the differing emotions that surface in the institution, and recognize the importance of positive attitudes in setting a tone that will permeate the organization.

Seven Key Leadership Skills for Faculty

For leadership in the professoriate to thrive, colleges and universities must actively encourage leadership within the faculty ranks. In addition, academic institutions must establish systems to promote and develop leadership skills among faculty. Some leadership skills in the professoriate are interchangeable at various levels in the administrative structure of the college or university. It is important to understand that it is not necessary for faculty to assume full-time positions. Rather, the focus of this discussion is that leadership in the professoriate can manifest itself in different ways in the college or university yet still provide positive, sustainable, and practical effects for all involved as well as for the organization.

Research supports the notion that many executive skills are transferable and that their effects are long lasting (Groysberg 2014). According to Groysberg (2014), the seven most needed and highest priority skills include leadership, strategic thinking and execution, technical and technology skills, team and relationship building, communication and presentation, change management, and integrity. If these skills are to be transferable to the professoriate, faculty—and ultimately organizations—must find a strategic path to reach both short- and long-term goals, with faculty assuming varied leadership roles on this pathway to success (Groysberg 2014). Groysberg (2014) also asserts that authenticity is a necessity for leadership roles. This authenticity is evident in professoriate leadership when faculty leaders balance the overarching mission and vision of the college or university with individual goals as well as the goals of individual departments. This authentic leadership builds trust among colleagues within small groups and the larger community of the college or university. Trust is built by showing respect for everyone, demonstrating ethical behavior, and becoming a resource that others consider indispensable.

Strategic thinking and execution relates to authenticity in leadership in that an effective, efficient faculty leader is able to synthesize and integrate resources to meet both departmental and institutional goals. Thus, the effective faculty leader mobilizes as many resources as are available and necessary to bring these goals to fruition. In this work, constant attention is given to maintaining the faculty leader's behaviors of strategic leadership (Reeves 2002). This thought process is directly linked to being attentive to the proposed mission, real-time information, and actual outcomes surrounding goal attainment. Consequently, these areas should be among the top priorities for leaders in the professoriate (Reeves 2002).

Technical and technology skills are critical assets for today's faculty leadership. Such skills necessarily include mastery of the ever-changing technology that allows for high-level teaching and learning. These skills also encompass the content knowledge as it applies to one's area of expertise. Thus, this technological know-how and ability enables the faculty leader to be at the forefront regarding how innovation continually affects the college or university's mission and vision.

Team and relationship building are always of critical importance in any organization. For the leader in the professoriate, the ability to build and guide a team toward the common goals of a department and an organization assumes that collegiality is the foundation. Collegiality is not something that is given; it is something that is earned. Faculty leaders, as previously mentioned, are often suspicious of colleagues who wish to assume leadership roles. This suspicion generally stems from the individual leader's desire to push his or her own agenda (Barden and Curry 2013). Groysberg (2014) refers to a leader as one who has the ability to lead others without using the title of leader, assuring that team members have the resources needed to be successful in their roles. Further, a leader is able to assume many different responsibilities at the same time to lead in an effective and efficient way (Groysberg 2014).

Groysberg (2014) also reinforces the idea that communication and presentation are critical skills for the faculty leader to possess. According to Groysberg (2014), the ability to articulate information and persuasively present one's positions on specific issues is important in order to be respected by colleagues as a leader. Clear and concise dissemination of information to various constituencies is a necessary component of this aspect of leadership. Because there is such diversity among the constituencies with which a leader in the professoriate interacts, communication may sometimes prove quite difficult. A leader's collaborative, knowledgeable, convincing, and friendly communication both within and outside the organization is essential to ensure success (Groysberg 2014).

The skill of implementing positive change management in what sometimes may be volatile situations with colleagues often proves to be a challenge for the faculty leader (Groysberg 2014). This essential change management skill set requires that the leader in the professoriate be adept at providing a safe, welcoming environment in which colleagues feel comfortable. Fostering such an inclusive environment will enable the faculty leader to build consensus more easily and also implement change that otherwise may seem too quick or not necessary (Groysberg 2014).

Groysberg (2014) concludes that integrity is the foundation of the true leader in the professoriate. Of course, building a reputation of integrity within and beyond an organization does not happen overnight. It must be painstakingly cultivated, especially with colleagues, day in and day out over a significant time period. Leaders in the professoriate will always have their behaviors and interactions scrutinized for authenticity, for outcomes, and for the underlying motivations to ensure that their actions are for the holistic good of the college or university. Consistently demonstrating behaviors that reflect unquestioned morals and ethics are at the center of this most important leadership skill (Groysberg 2014). Combined with the other skills sets described throughout this section, authentic professoriate leaders must possess unconditional commitment to the institution through their actions, not just their words. Without this demonstrated long-term commitment, the level of integrity needed to be a true leader will likely never be achieved.

Leadership: Will Professors Embrace the Challenge?

Considering the many skills necessary for leadership in the professoriate, the essential question remains: Will faculty expand their scholarly skills into the area of faculty leadership? Research suggests that given the appropriate, timely, and adequate resources to acquire and execute skills beyond the traditional role of the professoriate, faculty can become strong leaders in the college/university setting (Hill 2012). The resources needed to assist faculty members in reaching the leadership level in their respective fields vary considerably. Providing mutual assistance, which is sometimes referred to as team faculty pairings, is often included among these resources. A focus also should be placed on pilot programs that identify specific faculty members for leadership positions in an organization in a cross-disciplinary way (Hill 2012). Of course, in all this, administrators and professors alike must not lose sight of the academic nature of the professoriate and the importance of ongoing scholarship.

When promoting leadership in the professoriate, the process must be carefully planned, implemented, and executed. That being said, emphasizing the importance of mutual work embedded in the professoriate as well as establishing faculty pairings within and among departments become reasonable steps to take to enhance and advance leadership skills across an institution. These mutual pairings acknowledge the expertise and experience involved in the work toward attaining and facilitating leadership positions while simultaneously validating that the professoriate is indeed collaborative in nature. Faculty members thrive on interactions, discussions, and collaboration with one another; they also benefit by receiving regular feedback from their peers. Pairing faculty tapped for leadership in the professoriate builds an even firmer foundation, which helps all parties involved experience an added level of comfort and reliability

(Hill 2012). Faculty are expected to exchange ideas, research, and methodology as well as show the natural progression of how leadership skills translate into the professor's day-to-day work. The mutual pairings also assume that those seeking or identified for leadership positions in the professoriate have unique characteristics that can create a cross-pollination of skills between faculty members. This pairing should include exercises that promote leadership, such as role-playing in the realm of leadership, and the forthright sharing of ideas about challenges that may arise when leadership positions are eventually attained (Hill 2012).

As faculty increasingly include leadership functions in their roles, scholarship in a specific content area must still be emphasized and valued, as this has historically been the underpinning of the professoriate (Barden and Curry 2013). However, with the move toward greater leadership responsibilities in the professoriate, perhaps this scholarship should be expanded to include not only content-specific research but also research on leadership skills and how these leadership skills can effectively interface with the faculty's existing level of rigorous scholarship. Encouraging faculty to work on narrowly focused research regarding specific issues of leadership in the professoriate and how these issues translate into practical terms actually merges two skill sets. For research on leadership in the professoriate to be focused, the investigation should be narrowed down to major issues and have a specified timeline for discussion, final reporting, and implementation. This compartmentalizes the process and sets a concrete time for implementation of the leadership skills. This research assumes that professors are working in small, sometimes paired groups in a way that is comfortable for all participants and in an environment where faculty can engage in frank and meaningful dialogue. When this process is completed, faculty should be knowledgeable about leadership in the professoriate and hopefully feel ready to embrace the challenges of accepting such leadership roles (Hill 2012).

The final step of this process is to encourage professors to pursue leadership roles within the faculty ranks. Some research supports the use of pilot programs in professoriate leadership (Hill 2012). Pilot programs involve a small number of faculty who will undertake leadership roles, span a limited time frame (usually one to three years), and require the establishment of an evaluation process prior to their commencement to address any modifications that may be necessary along the way. This evaluation process further assures participating faculty members that their feedback regarding the pilot's implementation truly matters and will be used to improve the program going forward.

Great Leaders in the Professoriate

Are great leaders in the professoriate willing to significantly expand their role if resources are made available to them to advance to the leadership level? Research reveals that faculty do want to serve in leadership positions or have leadership responsibilities (Barden and Curry 2013). Many faculty think strategically, from a global and organizational level instead of autonomously; these professors understand the issues that directly affect an academic institution's mission and culture. Equipped with this overarching understanding, demonstrating a desire to contribute on a larger scale, and possessing skills to counter the current reality of the autonomous faculty member, the professoriate leader can use this strategic and organizational thinking to train others in this perspective.

Beyond encouragement, there must also be training for faculty to develop these leadership-focused strategic thinking skills that will enable them to think beyond themselves, their classrooms, and their students. This expansive viewpoint will raise awareness of the necessity of more global, institution-wide perspectives. Thus, leadership will take a stronger hold in the faculty ranks, and college/university boards will begin to realize that they now have the ability to look for true leaders among existing faculty members (Barden and Curry 2013).

These changes in the overall faculty mindset and the mindset of administrators on college and university campuses will not develop without both the administration and the professoriate becoming willing to take risks. Leading in the professoriate certainly has its challenges in contemporary higher education, and it will likely continue to as it evolves in the twenty-first century. One of the risks for the "scholar-leader" is to be willing to think and speak, even if it may be counter to the conventional faculty approach. An example of this type of courage and forward-thinking perspective is when faculty are able to move beyond their world of scholarship, teaching, and service in their own individual departments to engage in vision setting for the institution as a whole (Barden and Curry 2013). Boyatzis and McKee (2005) ask questions such as the following to encourage leaders to think beyond current practices: Do faculty leaders possess the skills to inspire others? Do they routinely have a positive viewpoint, even when facing challenges? Do faculty leaders connect well with the colleagues with whom they are collaborating as they lead? Do they truly understand what motivates professors to always work at their optimal level? Are faculty members really authentic when they attempt to take on institutional leadership roles? In answering such questions, there needs to be openness about continuing to focus on what is often termed a "moving target" when it comes to additional responsibilities in the professoriate. Often, the unexpected mandates are enough to push professors back into entrenchment mode, less willing to take risks to become faculty leaders (Boyatzis and McKee 2005). According to Boyatzis and McKee (2005), paying attention to all these pressures and taking adequate time for reflection will allow leaders in the professoriate to perform at a high level and not be as likely to regress to autonomy.

Another example of putting professoriate leadership into practice is replicating this leadership work at local, state, regional, national, and international levels through presentations at conferences. Leading professional development sessions to assist with training colleagues in the strategic thinking skills discussed earlier is also something a faculty leader can do. Of course, such leaders should continually model leadership skills within the organization. Further, when leaders in the professoriate display excitement for their work on campus by showing that they are willing to assume leadership roles, these behaviors communicate a very positive message to other faculty members and may even inspire or motivate them to do the same. Faculty members are attentive to the behaviors, work, and sense of culture in the organization. The positive attitudes and behaviors of professoriate leaders often raise other colleagues' levels of involvement in important ways across the entire college or university (Boyatzis and McKee 2005).

In addition, a quality leader in the professoriate will expand these daily positive behaviors to include the following: assuring that both departmental and institutional goals are attainable and directly linked to the mission of the organization, clarifying the plan of action for how to achieve these goals, ensuring that all faculty members are engaged and committed to contribute toward attaining these goals, consistently evaluating the ongoing work, and providing continuous feedback on faculty members' work as professors and potential leaders. A firm commitment to the goal-oriented action steps ensures a correlation between the college or university's overarching priorities and the daily work of the professoriate leaders as well as the other faculty, including those professors aspiring to become the institution's next leaders (Reeves 2002).

Consistent with these challenging activities are other related actions assumed by leaders in the professoriate. Such actions include participating in the development of the overall strategy to attain the vision of the college/university. It is also important that faculty leaders consistently communicate this vision and motivate colleagues so that they work toward this vision. A great professoriate leader will align faculty skills with specific ways to become involved in attaining the goals that fulfill this vision. Finally, a quality leader in the professoriate assists colleagues with opportunities to grow in their daily work and encourages other faculty to embrace leadership roles as well (Hill 2012).

Conclusion

Through careful planning, many successful leaders in academia can pool and leverage the resources currently available to them on their college or university campuses. Effective leadership teams are developed strategically, and considerable effort must be committed by all to the work of leadership development in the professoriate (Boyatzis and McKee 2005). Doing so will provide a new, more diverse face of leadership, with varying perspectives as institutions of higher education proactively make decisions; solve problems; and tackle contemporary, multifaceted issues. Now more than ever, the participation of faculty leaders is critical so that colleges and universities will continue to grow, prosper, and provide quality learning opportunities at every level of postsecondary education.

Points to Remember

- The definition of leadership in higher education formerly only included teaching and researching; however, this definition is continually changing and expanding as the needs of students and society change.
- Despite the shifting requirements of the professoriate, the university or college's mission and vision still remains the primary focus for professors.
- Strengths and weaknesses in leadership skills among faculty members must be recognized and addressed.
- The following abilities and attributes are among the specific leadership skill set needed for the professoriate: leadership, strategic thinking and execution, technical and technological

aptitude, team and relationship building, communication and presentation, change management, and integrity.

- Adequate resources as well as focused selection of faculty are necessary for successful leadership in the professoriate.
- For leadership in the professoriate to be successful, the mindset among administrators and faculty members at colleges and universities must be changed significantly.

References

Barden, D. M., and J. Curry. 2013, April 8. Faculty members can lead, but will they? *The Chronicle of Higher Education* 5(15). Retrieved from http://chronicle.com/article/Faculty-Members-Can-Lead-but/138343

Boyatzis, R., and A. McKee. 2005. *Resonant leadership: Renewing yourself and connecting with others through mindfulness, hope, and compassion.* Boston, MA: Harvard Business School Press.

Groysberg, B. 2014, March 18. The seven skills you need to thrive in the c-suite. *Harvard Business Review.* Retrieved from https://hbr.org/2014/03/the-seven-skills-you-need-to-thrive-in-the-c-suite

Hill, P. 2012, November/December. Online educational delivery models: A descriptive view. *EDUCAUSE Review* 47(6):85–97. Retrieved from http://er.dut.ac.za/bitstream/handle/123456789/56/Hill_2012_Online_Educational_Delivery_Models.pdf?sequence=1

Reeves, D. B. 2002. *The daily disciplines of leadership: How to improve student achievement, staff motivation, and personal organization.* San Francisco, CA: Wiley.

CHAPTER 6

Student Recruitment and Retention
Essential Faculty Contributions

By Judith L. Klimkiewicz

Introduction

More than 40 years ago, "the two R's" meant *rest* and *recuperation.* Now, the term adopts a deeper educational significance: recruitment and retention. Historically, college and university faculty members were not involved in, nor were they expected to play a role in, these two vital areas of postsecondary academia. Today, involving professors in the admissions and retention process can be critical to the higher education institution's success and livelihood. It is essential that colleges and universities find ways for faculty and administration to participate in these efforts by recruiting students who can succeed and then immersing them in programs that ensure degree completion with minimum disruption to their primary role as professors.

Globalization, with its accompanying socioeconomic, demographic, and technological changes, is having a significant impact on America's workforce and its postsecondary institutions. Ten years ago, 60% of jobs required some postsecondary education and training (Lotkowski, Robbins, and Noeth 2004). Forecasts of future educational demands to fill job growth by industry exhibit an ever-increasing need for an educated workforce. By 2020, 65% of all jobs will require some postsecondary education or training beyond high school (Carnevale, Smith, and Strohl 2013). Students now have more options than ever on their choice of college or technical institute. To continue to be viable, postsecondary institutions need to attract students that fit their particular academic and social environment and immerse those selected students in retention programs that are personalized and effective.

The Professor's Role in Admissions and Recruitment

With declining eligible student enrollment, both colleges and universities are under pressure to expand recruitment efforts to meet the necessary enrollment minimums. As a result, many admissions offices are asking faculty members to assist in recruitment efforts, which has created some difficulty because most professors see their role as exclusively involving teaching, conducting research, presenting their research at conferences, and other professional activities. Postsecondary faculty members, for the most part, do not understand their role in recruitment, nor do they believe that they should have to participate in the recruitment process. Successfully engaging professors in the recruitment process is a dilemma that many colleges and universities now face as they seek to attract new students. Professors are involved in a multitude of initiatives, including new program development, advising, and student orientation (Smith 2007); involving professors as partners in the recruitment and admissions process is equally important.

Benefits of Faculty Engagement

The quality of professors as teachers and mentors rates among the most important attributes for both students and parents when choosing a higher education institution (Stamats Communications 2006). Hence, interaction and encounters with faculty during the admissions process are critical. Holding small individual meetings, either in the admissions office or sometime during the initial recruitment process, enables students to interact with professors and create contacts that will benefit their postsecondary education experience as well as postgraduate employment. These meetings also often serve to "wake up" the student to the realization of the demands and expectations of the collegiate level, which they may not truly understand until these conferences take place.

By involving faculty in the admissions process, they truly begin to understand the challenges and rewards of new student enrollment (Carter, Lehman, and Tremblay 2008). In addition, having the professor actively participate in the recruitment process may help address complaints later on about the quality of the student in the classroom. One way to change the quality of the student is to have faculty involved in recruitment.

Building a Recruitment Team

The levels of interest in building recruitment teams will vary across college and university campuses, and it is important to note the benefits and challenges of being a member of such a team. Successful faculty involvement in this process often begins with a core of willing professors. Likely, these professors are the ones who have experienced declining enrollments or a decrease in the quality of the enrolled students. These professors typically have compelling motives and clear reasons for becoming involved in recruitment. Another effective contributor on a recruitment team is the professor who understands marketing and the importance of the branding of the college or university. He or she is often the legacy or alumnus member of the faculty who truly believes in the mission and vision of the institution. He or she "walks the walk" and "talks the talk" when advertising the high quality of the institution. Such a professor is an indispensable member of the recruitment team, always willing to express to prospective students the benefits of their attendance.

In addition, it is constructive to include faculty members on the recruitment team who have clearly earned widespread respect from students and achieved exceptionally high ratings in student surveys. Upperclass students on the recruitment team can identify faculty members who would be effective agents in student recruitment. Information on how certain faculty interact with students and demonstrate sincere support for student success also can be obtained from student staff, who often are willing to share their opinions about their professors.

Finally, college and university administrators must provide both emotional and financial support by encouraging and rewarding the faculty recruitment team in various ways. In a 2003 study, more than three-quarters of faculty respondents (78.3%) indicated that the administration did not reward them for their assistance in recruiting undergraduate students (Pollack 2003). Many of these professors noted that although small rewards, such as free lunches, gift certificates, pins, and sporting event tickets, were kind gestures on the part of administrators, they were insufficient compensation for an important student recruitment task (Pollack 2003). More significant to most faculty members was the lack of concrete awards (Carter et al. 2008; Pollack 2003). Faculty members listed the following as more acceptable examples of recognition for their student recruitment efforts: more release time, merit pay, college service, and consideration during the tenure process (Carter et al. 2008).

Recruitment initiatives during this era of declining postsecondary student enrollment could involve professors in a nearly full-time effort. Obviously, having faculty perform full-time recruitment is not a realistic or viable approach; therefore, each postsecondary institution must seriously consider the needs, interest levels, and commitment requirements of its professors before moving forward with faculty-based recruitment teams.

Suggestions for Faculty Involvement

Professors play a critical role in recruiting students. Their involvement is necessary but difficult to acquire in the best of circumstances. Experts in postsecondary recruiting recommend the following best practices to engage faculty in the process:

- Have faculty participate in the campus visit program.
- Encourage faculty to make off-campus visits to high school classrooms.
- Involve faculty in scholarship or hiring committees.
- Have faculty assist with prospective student e-mail or letter campaigns.
- Use faculty services as instructors during precollege programs.
- Feature faculty profiles on recruitment websites.
- Request faculty input during the preparation of marketing materials.
- Invite faculty members to speak at recruitment events. (Carter et al. 2008)

Focused events, such as open houses and departmental orientations, that concentrate exclusively on prospective students and their parents are the most effective (Barnds 2011). At these events, professors should be encouraged to distribute their business cards so that students and parents can contact them directly (Barnds 2011; Hoover 2011). Featuring current students or alumni at such events to add to the institution's overall message and provide clear examples of future success to prospective students is also an effective approach. Involving future undergraduates with hands-on activities, either in classroom or social settings, better prepares them to become a part of the organization.

Information is a powerful tool when recruiting, so using a survey or questionnaire is highly recommended to obtain critical personal information about the prospective student (Hoover 2011). The questionnaire should be brief and to the point. Discovering the individual student's passions, likes, and dislikes can only aid in future recruitment stages.

Finally, recruitment teams must never forget the benefit of personalization and customization (Barnds 2011). The negative impact of a lack of personalization in e-mails or letters cannot be underestimated. "If you want something to matter to a student, it is critical to personalize and customize. An example of doing this is the handwritten note on each offer of admission and the customized paragraph within each letter that highlights why a student caught our attention is critical" (Barnds 2011, 1). For example, Harvard University sends a personal note to its newly admitted students. If Harvard, which possibly experiences the fewest recruitment problems, finds this initiative highly effective, it is only logical that other postsecondary institutions facing far more serious recruitment concerns would benefit from this practice as well.

The Institution's Role on Student Retention

First-year college students in U.S. higher education today are more likely to leave their initial institution than stay and complete their degree (Cuseo 2012). According to Tinto (2006; 2007), postsecondary students who attend multiple institutions take longer on average to finish their degree. Only 34% of students who attended three or more higher education institutions had earned a degree after six years (Aud, Hussar, Kena, Bianco, Frolich, Kemp, and Tahan 2011). In short, approximately 40 of every 100 college/university entrants will depart the higher education system without earning any type of degree (Tinto 1993; 2006; 2007). Student retention rates at both two- and four-year institutions have been declining steadily since the mid-1960s (Aud et al. 2011; Tinto 1993; 2006; 2007).

From the perspective of the institution, improving student retention rates starts with a thorough review of the possible causes behind student attrition. Practices that retain students are learned at the institutional level, using a multistep process that begins with determining, storing (in a database), and analyzing student characteristics; this information is then used to identify the at-risk students who are more likely to drop out as well as to develop effective, efficient intervention methods to retain them (Delen 2011). According to Tinto's extensive research on student retention published in textbooks (1987; 1993), the fundamental reasons for students deciding to leave college are complex and involve both the learner and the institution:

Though the intention and commitments with which individuals enter college matter, what goes on after entry matters more. It is the daily interaction of the personnel with other members of the college in both formal and informal academic and social domains of the college, and it's in the student's perceptions or evaluation of the interactions that in large measure determine decisions as to staying or leaving. ... Student retention is at least as much a function of institutional behavior as it is of student behavior. (1987, 127, 177)

Because of the complexity of the interactions of variables that cause students to drop out of college, advanced analysis in the form of various data mining methods are used to identify the most important of a large number of contributing variables. Using a combination of artificial neural network and decision tree analysis of a large student database for a six-year period at a large Midwestern university, Delen (2011) determined that precollege educational performance, first-year undergraduate performance, and financial resources were strong indicators of students being retained for their next year at the institution.

The Faculty's Influence on Student Retention

The largest problem in contemporary American higher education is often not recruiting the student into the institution but rather retaining the student. Most colleges and universities recognize the importance of retention, but few acknowledge the reality that the one form of institutional behavior that most influences student retention is the behavior or actions of its professors (Tinto 2007). Many instructors do not realize how much they may influence a student's desire to stay, but the reality of the professor's role is obvious. Many faculty members are still under the impression that students drop out because of personal or financial reasons or academic deficiencies, not as a result of inadequate socialization of the student into the culture of the institution. According to extensive research conducted since the 1960s on student retention and summarized by Aljohani (2016), institutional involvement matters, and it matters most during the student's first critical year of college. As a result, much of the early practice focused on the first year of college, especially the transition to college, and the nature of student contact with faculty, most notably outside the classroom. There was a rush to implement services ranging from first-year experience activities and extended orientation to first-year student seminars/courses and tailored extracurricular programs.

Tinto (2007) later observed that faculty members are not regularly trained and instructed to teach as all educators at lower levels are, nor are professors required to obtain certifications. As a result, it is important to offer faculty development programs dedicated to both improving their teaching skills and strengthening their understanding of the importance of social integration of new students into the fabric and culture of the institution.

The effect of faculty on student retention is quite dramatic when one considers the number of areas in college life that faculty influence (Cuseo 2012). Consider, for example, the number of times per week a professor sees or interacts with a student both in and out of class. The additional influence on time away from the class can be even more dramatic; homework, reading assignments, online correspondence, etc., all directly impact the student outside of the classroom countless times throughout a semester (Cuseo 2012).

Of course, faculty members are responsible for assessing, evaluating, and grading student work. This particularly sensitive area is often the most serious of all student-faculty contact. The poor evaluation of a student's work often sends him or her on the road to anger, low motivation, and a loss of self-esteem—all attributes a professor hopes are short-lived. Unfortunately, for many students, particularly the academically weaker ones, earning a poor grade may be enough of a negative experience to cause withdrawal from both the class and the college or university (Cuseo 2012).

Because of their frequent contact with students, faculty members are in the best position to identify issues or warning signs for student disengagement. Hence, professors are uniquely poised to recommend an intervention or refer students to seek additional support services, which could be critically important for student success. In this way, faculty plays a crucial role in student retention.

Faculty Strategies that Promote Student Retention

Given the mounting research supporting the connection between effective faculty involvement and student retention, the remainder of this chapter will focus on strategies college and university professors can implement that are strongly correlated to higher rates of student retention. Understandably, the size of the professor's student load, number of classes taught, and rules of the institution will influence the availability and success of these recommended strategies, but many faculty members will likely be able to adopt one or more of the following practices.

The chilling fact is that less than 60% of students entering four-year colleges in America today will graduate within six years (Bowen, Chingos, and MacPherson 2009). Minority students will have an even more difficult time earning a college degree. For many years, the common view among faculty was that there would always be students who should fail and who indeed ultimately do. Many such "old-school" faculty did not care to keep track of dwindling enrollments, nor did they think that retention was an expectation, let alone an urgent requirement, of their job.

According to Tinto (2006), fostering students ranks as the most important condition for student retention. Hence, the importance of the role professors' play in student retention is quite evident. What can faculty members do to encourage retention? They can set high expectations and provide the support necessary to achieve them. They can create robust opportunities for students to be actively involved in class. In addition, professors can teach the strategies necessary to be successful in the particular subject by integrating various learning and study techniques into their courses.

According to the 2009 National Survey of Student Engagement (NSSE), there are five benchmarks of effective practice that can be used to measure student engagement and satisfaction at baccalaureate institutions:

- Level of academic challenge
- Active and collaborative learning
- Student-faculty interaction
- Enriching educational experiences
- Supportive campus environment

The researchers concluded that there is a direct correlation between student satisfaction, engagement in meaningful learning activities, and retention (NSSE 2009).

The NSSE also produced a paper entitled *What Faculty Members Can Do* (Kinzie 2005) detailing effective faculty strategies and practices that were culled from an extensive study of schools with higher than predicted graduation rates. According to the study, faculty can implement the following strategies to promote student success:

- Embrace undergraduates and their learning by supporting academic and developmental growth. Seek to develop students' talents and learn how to support students who are underprepared academically.
- Set and maintain high expectations for student performance. However, make sure all expectations are appropriate to where students are developmentally and academically.
- Clarify what students need to know to be successful.
- Use engaging approaches to teaching that take into consideration students' abilities and learning styles.
- Build on students' knowledge, talents, and abilities.
- Provide meaningful feedback to students.
- Weave diversity into the curriculum.
- Make time for students.
- Hold students accountable for their share. (Kinzie 2005)

Faculty Mentoring

Historically, professors were not expected to play a major role in retaining students; rather, their job was to sort students by assigning grades and opinions of their work without worrying about their failure (Magna Publications 2010). Postsecondary institutions have steadily increased the number of faculty-student mentoring programs since the late 1990s (Walker and Taub 2001). The availability of these faculty role models is incredibly valuable for all students, particularly for vulnerable first-year or underrepresented students. Research indicates that there is an undeniable link between student mentoring and retention (Coley, Coley, and Lynch-Holmes 2016). The complication most colleges and universities face is the inability to have a one-to-one relationship between the faculty member and a student. Research results show that the "network" mentoring programs in which multiple students are mentored by one faculty/ staff member are comparable in effectiveness to the one-to-one dyadic (Soria 2012; Walker and Taub 2001). Student satisfaction increased because of the quality and frequency of the student contact with the mentor, even when the contact occurred in group situations rather than in one-to-one meetings (Soria 2012; Walker and Taub 2001). If this is so, one must then wonder what the difference is between mentoring and advising, where the caseload is often multiple students and not one-on-one guidance. Furthermore, research on student perception of advisees points to the conclusion that students must value advisors who serve as mentors for the arrangement to be effective (Coley et al. 2016; Gordon and Habley 2000; Kuh, Kinzie, Schuh, and Whitt 2010). Understandably, mentoring is a key element of effective college advisement and student retention.

Conditions that Increase Retention

According to distinguished Syracuse University education professor Vincent Tinto (2006; 2013; 2014), many colleges and universities discuss the importance of retention, and some even devote vast resources, employ full-time consultants, or design first-year engagement programs to guide incoming students in their transition. Nevertheless, most institutions of higher education do not take student retention seriously enough. Colleges and universities have done little to adapt the retention measures to a changing student candidate population; hence, most postsecondary institutions currently need to address the deeper root causes of student attrition (Tinto 2006; 2013; 2014). Tinto (2013) uses Newton's First Law of Motion, a scientific principle introduced in 1687, to clarify the measures universities need to take to improve student retention. Simply stated, the First Law of Motion means that a body at rest will stay at rest, while a body in motion will continue in motion until influenced by an external force. Tinto (2013) explains that momentum is necessary for student success, and gaining momentum is the key to student retention and, ultimately, student completion. Certain intermediate points of attainment, or momentum points, include the timely completion of coursework, timely declaration of a major, earning a number of degree credit hours within a particular period of time, and completion to earn a degree or certificate. A student who attains these intermediate completion points within the time frames expected is far more likely to complete his or her required degree curriculum. Many institutions have focused on first-year efforts to acclimate students and encourage classroom success early on, but these institutions have paid little attention to helping students gain momentum so that they move quickly through their degree programs in successive years. Institutions should present students with coherent course pathways from their first day on campus through degree completion by providing measures that promote momentum from first-year through graduation (Tinto 2013).

To do more to promote retention for all students, colleges must move beyond add-on services and integrate sound educational environments into the very fiber of the institution.

Fortunately, recent research clearly indicates that at the college level, the nature of the educational environment in which students find themselves, rather than the qualities of the students themselves, promotes retention (Tinto 2006; 2013). Administrators can change their institution's existing conditions if they are serious about increasing their rates of student retention.

Tinto (2006; 2013), who is extensively cited in this chapter, has studied college retention for over four decades. He has conducted research and has written widely about student retention and the role faculty members play in it. He offers five main conditions (i.e., expectations, advice, support, involvement, and learning) that help faculty members support student retention:

- Expect students to succeed.
- Provide students with clear, consistent information about institutional requirements as well as effective advising about programs of study and career goals.
- Provide academic, social, and personal support.
- Involve students as valued members of the institution.
- Foster learning. (Tinto 2006)

The following is an expansion of each of these five conditions that Tinto (2006) considers to be the ideal attributes that will bring postsecondary institutions one step closer to creating the ideal environment for student retention.

First, students at both small and large postsecondary institutions are more likely to persist and graduate in settings where those in authority hold high expectations and demand more from them (Coley et al. 2016; Tinto 2006). Very few educators can point to great success stories of turnaround schools, which increased their enrollment, retention, or graduation rates, that did not hold their students to higher standards and expectations.

Second, students are more likely to remain until graduation in environments that provide clear and consistent information about institutional requirements through effective advising (Tinto 2006). A great advisor not only advises students on required courses and obligations but also guides them to future aspirations after college. Most students enter college undecided about which major to declare or unsure of their career pathway, and such students need instructions from that special advisor to guide them toward the correct path.

Third, many students, especially those in their first year of college, require academic, social, and personal support throughout their undergraduate experience (Tinto 2006). Colleges provide this assistance in many ways. Some arrange for summer bridge programs, mentoring opportunities, student clubs, or daily meetings with faculty. Regardless of the delivery system, the available support needs to be known by students to be effective.

Fourth, as in any organization, one must feel valued by the community (Tinto 2006). Students, regardless of race, ethnicity, or gender must believe themselves to be an important part of the institution no matter its size. Colleges must work to involve all members of the student body effectively, particularly in that first year when students' attachment to their college is so weak (Soria 2012; Tinto 2006).

The fifth and final condition essential for student retention is the fostering of learning (Tinto 2006). "Learning has always been the key to student retention" (Tinto 2006, 3). Colleges and universities that are successful in developing environments that encourage learning are successful in retaining their students. Experiencing the joy of learning and being actively involved in the educational process connects individual students to their faculty, their classmates, and ultimately their college.

Conclusion

Despite extensive research on student recruitment, persistence, and retention, the level of student attrition has not improved significantly over the past 30 years (Braxton, Brier, and Steele 2007). The reality is that most postsecondary institutional efforts have not translated into substantial growth in student retention and graduation rates (Tinto 2006; 2014).

Involving professors in the recruitment and retention of students can be critical to the success of the institution. Admissions, recruitment, and retention professionals are acutely aware of the various events that can multiply their efforts, such as open houses, orientations, college fairs, advertising, and first-year experience programs, among others. Personal connections with faculty, both before enrollment as well as within and outside the classroom, are vital for all students to succeed in their pursuit of a college degree. Overall, faculty involvement is a critical component of the recruitment efforts at any postsecondary institution. The type, depth, and length of the faculty-student recruitment experience prior to college selection are essential keys to future success. If the recruitment relationship is unsuccessful, the top-notch students and the students appropriate for the institution either do not select that college/university or eventually leave because they do not feel connected enough to the institution to stay. If the recruitment relationship is successful, the student enrolls and, given the proper retention environment, stays enrolled through successful completion and graduation. One should always remember that there is no single blueprint for success (Kuh et al. 2010). However, faculty, through their roles in recruitment and retention initiatives, are essential to achieving positive student outcomes (Lorenzetti 2013). As Tinto states, student retention through program completion requires great effort:

> Improvement in institutional rates of student success does not arise by chance. It is not simply the result of good intentions; although good intentions are clearly a requirement, improvement in rates of student success requires more. It requires an intentional, structured, and coherent set of policies and actions that coordinate the work of many programs and people across campus, actions that are sustained and scaled up over time and to which resources are allocated. There is no magic cure to improvement. It simply takes time and sustained effort. (2014, 6)

Points to Remember

- Historically, college faculty members were not involved in, nor were they expected to play a role in, student recruitment and retention.
- With declining student enrollment, colleges and universities are under pressure to expand recruitment efforts to meet the necessary enrollment numbers to ensure institutional viability.
- Today, involving faculty in the admissions and retention processes can be critical to the institution's academic success and financial stability.
- Faculty engagement and faculty mentoring rank among the most important attributes for both parents and students when selecting a college (Coley et al. 2016; Soria 2012).

- First-year college students are more likely to leave their initial institution than stay and complete their degree (Cuseo 2012).
- Practices that retain students are learned at the institutional level.
- Many instructors do not realize how much they influence a student's desire to stay, but the reality is obvious.
- Institutional involvement matters for student retention, and it matters most in the critical first year of college.

References

Aljohani, O. 2016. A comprehensive review of the major studies and theoretical models of student retention in higher education. *Higher Education Studies* 6(2):1–18.

Aud, S., W. Hussar, G. Kena, K. Bianco, L. Frolich, J. Kemp, and K. Tahan. 2011. *The Condition of Education 2011* (NCES 2011-003). Washington, DC: U.S. Government Printing Office, U.S. Department of Education, National Center for Education Statistics.

Barnds, W. K. 2011, September 15. "Best practices" for departmental/faculty involvement in student recruitment and admissions. *Commentary about higher education and college admissions.* Retrieved from https://bowtieadmission.wordpress.com/2011/09/15/%e2%80%9cbest-practices%e2%80%9d-for-departmentalfaculty-involvement-in-student-recruitment-admissions-highered/

Bowen, W. G., M.M. Chingos, and M.S. MacPherson. 2009. *Crossing the finish line: Completing college at America's public universities.* Princeton University Press: Princeton, NJ.

Braxton, J. M., E.M. Brier, and S.L. Steele. 2007. Shaping retention from research to practice. *Journal of College Student Retention: Research, Theory, and Practice* 9(3):377–399.

Carnevale, A. P., N. Smith, and J. Strohl. 2013. *Recovery: Projections of jobs and education requirements through 2020.* Washington, DC: Center for Education and the Workforce, Georgetown Public Policy Institute, Georgetown University.

Carter, A., J. Lehman, and C. Tremblay. 2008, February. Engaging faculty in undergraduate recruitment: Perspectives, suggestions, and tips. *Strategic Enrollment Management (SEM) Source Newsletter.*

Coley, C., T. Coley, and K. Lynch-Holmes. 2016. *Retention and student success: Implementing strategies that make a difference* (Ellucian White Paper Series). Fairfax, VA: Ellucian. Retrieved from http://www.ellucian.com/White-Papers/Retention-and-student-success/

Cuseo, J. B. 2012. *The role of college faculty in promoting student retention: Instructional strategies for reducing student attrition.* Retrieved from http://uwc.edu/sites/uwc.edu/files/imce-uploads/employees/academic-resources/esfy/_files/role_of_college_faculty_in_promoting_student_retention_-_instructional_strategies_for_reducing_student_attrition.pdf

Delen, D. 2011. Predicting student attrition with data mining methods. *Journal of College Student Retention* 13(1):17–25.

Gordon, V. N., and W.R. Habley. 2000. *Academic advising: A comprehensive handbook.* San Francisco: Jossey-Bass.

Hoover, E. 2011, September 23. What, me, recruit? I'm a professor! *The Chronicle of Higher Education*. Retrieved from http://www.chronicle.com/blogs/headcount/what-me-recruit-im-a-professor/28821

Kinzie, J. 2005. *Promoting student success: What faculty members can do* (Occasional Paper No. 6). Bloomingdale, IN: Indiana University Center for Postsecondary Research. Retrieved from http://nsse.indiana.edu/institute/documents/briefs/DEEP%20Practice%20Brief%206%20What%20Faculty%20Members%20Can%20Do.pdf

Kuh, G. D., J. Kinzie, J.H. Schuh, and E.J. Whitt. 2010. *Student success in college: Creating conditions that matter*. San Francisco: Jossey-Bass.

Lorenzetti, J. P. 2013. Tips for involving faculty in recruitment and retention efforts. *Recruitment and Retention in Higher Education* [Newsletter]. Madison, WI: Magna Publications. Retrieved from http://www.magnapubs.com/newsletter/recruitment-retention/99/tips_for_involving_faculty_in_recruitment_and_retention_efforts-10700-1.html

Lotkowski, V. A., S.B. Robbins, and R.J. Noeth. 2004. *The role of academic and nonacademic factors in improving college retention* (ACT Policy Report). Iowa City, IA: ACT.

Pollack, K. 2003, December. Undergraduate student recruitment: The role of the faculty. *Strategic Enrollment Management (SEM) Source Newsletter*.

National Survey of Student Engagement (NSSE). 2009. *Promoting engagement for all students: The imperative to look within: 2008 Results*. Bloomington, IN: Indiana University Center for Postsecondary Research. Retrieved from http://nsse.indiana.edu/NSSE_2008_Results/docs/withhold/NSSE2008_Results_revised_11-14-2008.pdf

Smith, C. 2007. Finding the academic context: Involving faculty in strategic enrollment management. *College and University* 82(3):39–40.

Soria, K. M. 2012. Advising satisfaction: Implications for first-year students' sense of belonging and student retention. *The Mentor: An Academic Advising Journal*. Retrieved from https://dus.psu.edu/mentor/2012/10/advising-satisfaction/

Stamats Communications. 2006. *TeensTALK®: A review of college-bound teen trends, attitudes, lifestyles, and knowledge*. Cedar Rapids, IA: Author.

Tinto, V. 1987. *Leaving college: Rethinking the causes and cures for student attrition*. Chicago: University of Chicago Press.

Tinto, V. 1993. *Leaving college: Rethinking the causes and cures of student attrition*. 2nd ed. Chicago: University of Chicago Press.

Tinto, V. 2006. Research and practice of student retention: What next? *Journal of College Student Retention: Research, Theory, and Practice* 8(1):1–19.

Tinto, V. 2007. Taking student retention seriously: Rethinking the first year of college. Retrieved from http://nhcuc.org/pdfs/Taking_Student_Retention_Seriously.pdf

Tinto, V. 2013. Isaac Newton and student college completion. *Journal of College Student Retention* 15(1):1–7.

Tinto, V. 2014. Reflective practice: Tinto's South Africa lectures. *Journal of Student Affairs in Africa* 2(2):5–28.

Walker, S. C., and D.J. Taub. 2001. Variables correlated with satisfaction with a mentoring relationship in first-year college students and their mentors. *Journal of the First-Year Experience and Students in Transition* 13(1):47–67.

CHAPTER 7

Professors as Catalysts
Connecting College with Community

By Linda E. Denault

Introduction

In today's highly globalized and technologically advanced society, the professoriate faces many new challenges, particularly in terms of authenticity. Thus, it is important for professors in all disciplines to look for new or additional ways to make their courses more relevant. One way to achieve such necessary real-world applications of coursework is to connect the college experience to the community through meaningful interactions that will advance students' education and increase their potential for future success in a global economy.

Historical Perspective

Connecting college and community is certainly not a novel idea, but it is one whose time truly has come. There is an ancient Hebrew proverb by an unknown author that stands the test of time, as it speaks to every generation. Likely, its original intent was to serve as advice to parents regarding the rearing of their children, but it holds an important message for all educators as well: "Do not confine your children to your own learning, for they were born in another time." These words could not ring more true than right now in the twenty-first century as academia tries to provide a college education that meets the needs of the digital natives. Daggett reminds the educational community of the need to "focus on preparing students for their future instead of our past" (2008, 10). Daggett further explains that "a quality education prepares students to enter the global economy with the ability to apply what they learned in school to situations that they cannot foresee before graduating" (2008, 10).

For members of today's college community, that ancient Hebrew proverb serves as a reminder that in the hallowed halls of higher education, professors must be prepared to serve a new generation of students who are connected to one another and the world in ways previously unimagined even in the recent past. In light of this, the connection between college and community must take on new, broader meanings and applications to meet the changing needs of modern students, as a college education remains the most promising gateway to a successful future, and how colleges deliver that education may hold the key to students' reaching their professional and personal goals.

Historically, society has viewed colleges and universities as the centers of thought where new ideas often originate. For our current society, Wagner (2012) stresses the need for secondary schools and colleges to prepare today's students to become innovators. If America wants to remain competitive, innovation is deemed a prerequisite for success in the global knowledge economy of the twenty-first century (Friedman and Mandelbaum 2011). In his research, Wagner (2012) found that the culture of innovation is more atypical than typical on campuses across the country, and one of the missing ingredients is collaboration in solving real-world, interdisciplinary problems. Wagner supports his assertion by sharing the following message from an interview he conducted with Judy Gilbert, the talent director at Google: "Learning to solve problems across disciplinary boundaries is one of the most important things that schools can teach students to prepare them to work at companies like Google" (2012, 67). Meshing college and the business community through special, problem-based connections could provide a means for this type of learning to occur.

A Contemporary View

Postsecondary institutions need to offer a contemporary education to this millennial generation. College professors must recognize that students are not merely passive consumers of knowledge, regurgitating lecture notes for exams; rather, students ought to be called upon to apply the skills and knowledge acquired within real-world settings. Referencing Olin College in Needham, Massachusetts, as an example, Wagner (2012) shares information he gained from interviews of students working with a model of persistence used at a highly successful and innovative consulting and design firm called IDEO, whose motto is to fail early and often. An Olin student may have the opportunity to design his or her own curriculum, working on the solution to a proposed interdisciplinary problem within a real-world setting. The proposed solution to the problem usually undergoes several iterations before success is found, allowing this project to evolve across several courses. Clearly, a curriculum designed in this manner is highly motivating and ideal to include on a student's résumé.

Despite observable differences unique to the millennial generation, today's students still pursue postsecondary education for many of the same reasons that previous generations have sought a college degree. *The American Freshman: National Norms* (2011), developed by the Cooperative Institutional Research Program at the Higher Education Research Institute at UCLA, showed that incoming college students were more studious, but their top reason for attending college was to improve their prospect of obtaining a job upon graduation (Profile of the American Freshman 2012). For institutions of higher education to fulfill this student goal, courses must become more twenty-first century oriented. College and university programs must become better connected to the real world and more community based in the application of skills and knowledge taught within the classroom.

The rising costs associated with higher education today is another serious factor for consideration. In that same recent survey of college freshmen referenced previously, the challenge of financing a postsecondary education was noted as a major concern (Profile of the American Freshman 2012). Despite questions raised about the value of a college education, particularly in terms of "getting one's money's worth," entering college freshmen continue to view improving their job prospects as one of the chief reasons for obtaining their degree (Profile of the American Freshman 2012). What exactly do students need if their degrees are truly to open the doors of prospective employers for them? The standard line, which has become cliché, is that students need twenty-first century skills to succeed.

Twenty-First Century Skills

Definitions vary, but the National Council of Teachers of English's (NCTE's) *Literacies Framework* (2013) outlines a set of skills deemed essential for success in college, career, and the twenty-first century workplace. These skills are relatively broad in nature, which gives them appropriate flexibility to be relevant to a wide range of fields of study:

- Build intentional cross-cultural connections and relationships with others so as to pose and solve problems collaboratively and strengthen independent thought

- Develop proficiency and fluency with the tools of technology
- Design and share information for global communities to meet a variety of purposes
- Manage, analyze, and synthesize multiple streams of simultaneous information
- Create, critique, analyze, and evaluate multimedia texts
- Attend to the ethical responsibilities required by these complex environments. (NCTE 2013, as cited in Latham, Gross, and Witte 2013)

At the collegiate level, how can these NCTE (2013) skills be incorporated? *Intentional* is a term often used to describe the connections that college courses and programs must imbed to meet the needs of today's student body. This concept of intentionality necessitates that professors become less independent and autonomous and more willing to collaborate with colleagues—not only within their own departments but across disciplines and even into the community as well—to thoroughly plan the projects and products that would represent the culmination of this work. Such collaboration can result in the formulation of partnerships that will provide students with the hands-on training necessary for advancement of skills and, equally important, the relevance to classroom studies.

By incorporating these twenty-first century skills into a solid liberal arts foundation across the curriculum, often through general education requirements, today's students will acquire an educational foundation that will prepare them to adapt successfully to life on an ever-changing global stage. According to Pink (2006), the twenty-first century represents a progression from the information age to the conceptual age, with its emphasis on creativity and interpersonal skills. This view is aligned well to the skills named by the NCTE (2013) and to the shift in emphasis of the revised Bloom's taxonomy with problem solving, entrepreneurship, and communication considered central to success in today's economy.

Given what one may call a paradigm shift in skill emphasis, taking into account exactly how each college-level course or program will incorporate these essential twenty-first century skills becomes paramount. To build this foundation for the future and to be certain that student engagement is maximized, the professoriate needs to examine not only curriculum content but pedagogy as well. This emphasis reflects a recognition that contemporary education must focus on the learner and on making learning experiences more authentic. Bolstering this idea of colleges challenging the learner to go beyond being a mere consumer of the wisdom professors impart, Beckem and Watkins cite the 2008 research of Robert Kelley at Carnegie Mellon University, who found that within 10 years of the predominance of the Internet, "90% of the skills needed by today's knowledge workers are experiential" (2012, 61).

The Professoriate's Role

Part of the issue of keeping up with a fast-paced society comes in the need to break old habits, not just at the college level but also throughout K–16. Many times, students who enroll in teacher education programs arrive with a mindset already formed regarding the expectations of a classroom teacher. This mindset is based on their own prior experiences in the classroom, and it will be molded further by their field placements for student teaching. Unless the models these students see, both in the college classroom and in the field, demonstrate authentic learning activities that connect classroom, community, technology, and multiple disciplines, then the traditional pedagogical model will be perpetuated. "Teachers need to become adaptive experts who continually expand their expertise rather than maintain their status quo as routine experts" (Latham 2013, 63).

In adapting to a changing world, community links can be particularly important in the field of educator preparation, where understanding various cultures can be critical in promoting students' academic achievement. Preservice teaching programs need to give more attention to this area and incorporate goals for cultural understanding into the curriculum. Given the ever-expanding opportunities for interaction with others all over the world, beyond the deep discipline knowledge that has always been necessary, "teachers need to know how to foster cultural competence, emotional awareness, and leadership skills to facilitate not just interactions, but meaningful interactions and relationships" (Kereluik, Mishra, Fahnoe, and Terry 2013, 133).

An interesting example of a college program that attempts to meet today's challenges for teacher education and cultural awareness is the Bilingual Education Program at Chicago State University (Skinner 2010). This program, called the Grow Your Own Teachers initiative, was established initially with federal funds to provide support of a "consortia consisting of a community-based organization, a college of education, and a school district to recruit and prepare community leaders to become teachers" (Skinner 2010, 156).

Recognizing the demand for teachers skilled in working in high-need districts, particularly those with significant poverty and diversity, the Grow Your Own Teachers model sought to educate parents within the community to become teachers in their own local schools. Although only small numbers have completed the program, it does "suggest that urban schools can be improved from the inside out" (Tyack and Cuban 1995, as cited in Skinner 2010, 157) and may provide a model for other urban colleges and school districts to consider.

In light of the need to develop relevant skills for all learners, the importance of colleges connecting directly to the wider community (e.g., with schools, small businesses, the municipal services industry, health care organizations, nonprofits, and the like) cannot be overemphasized. Providing opportunities for college students to apply their skills and knowledge directly in real-world settings is central to the mission of colleges and universities today, addressing not only the issue of relevance but of rigor as well.

The Impact of Connected Learning on the Brain

As Daggett, a leading proponent of infusing rigor and relevance into the curriculum of American higher education, points out, "a curriculum that is both rigorous and relevant provides the tools students will need in order to be flexible when facing as yet unknown challenges of tomorrow" (2008, 10). In recognition of how individuals learn, the types of engaging, authentic projects that students accomplish through college-community connections can help establish the type of rich learning environment that has a positive impact on brain stimulation.

Leading brain expert Eric Jensen (2009) reminds educators that neuroplasticity allows changes to occur in the brain in response to experiences; the brain's structure and organization is more fluid than once believed. Jensen contends that "during periods of intense learning, students may experience increases in gray matter of 1% to 3% in the areas of the brain most involved with their studies" (2009, 48). Therefore, creating relevant, rigorous learning experiences via various college-community partnerships may have a significantly positive impact on brain activity.

In terms of brain stimulation and growth, using the theory of multiple intelligences (MI) for differentiation of instruction is another way for the college professor to connect to the real world and provide the flexibility that will be necessary for students to perform successfully in a global society (McFarlane 2011). Part of this stimulation can come from the way the professor organizes class activities and allows students to connect and collaborate on meaningful projects. Use of the MI theory also allows for greater recognition of individual differences. "Multiple intelligences … caters to the diversity characterizing individuals, and hence leads to a more effective and sensible approach to address unique learners in the classroom" (McFarlane 2011, 3). However, application of this theory is not necessarily reflected in the typical teacher-centered classroom.

Even in the second decade of the twenty-first century, the status quo in many colleges is the traditional classroom, reflecting a teacher-centered model rather than a student-centered model. Representative of the paradigm shift in education to a focus on the learner, the student-centered model is preferred and often used in conjunction with a team-based pedagogy that incorporates small, collaborative group work rooted in authentic tasks (Laist 2013). "An authentically engaging classroom will provide students with something to be engaged in. Team-based learning and project-based learning are effective precisely to the degree that they cultivate this fusion of individual motivation to establish a unique kind of expertise with the group objective of accomplishing a collective task" (Laist 2013, 13).

Outreach by the Professoriate

In terms of real-world experiences as part of a degree program, colleges and universities have traditionally offered practicum experiences for areas such as nursing and teaching. In these specialized fields, students train in a hospital setting or an elementary/secondary classroom as part of their degree program to fulfill requirements that will ultimately lead to licensure in their respective fields. However, recognizing the value of experiential learning that links postsecondary students to the real world will help ensure that some type of field experience will become an integral part of every major. Forward-thinking professors should advocate for increasing such field experiences.

Within the framework of community service learning (CSL) and community-based research (CBR), there are also opportunities for global connections that, when woven into the field experience, greatly enrich students' hands-on learning. Dating back to President George W. Bush's "points of light" (Points of Light 2016), and even earlier with President John F. Kennedy's inaugural address challenging citizens with a call to action, community service has been a mark of American culture. At the collegiate level, community connections through service have often been handled as voluntary, extracurricular functions organized through student clubs and other campus groups with a focus strictly on the service component. However, incorporating a classroom component could easily turn this specialized service into CSL.

One example of community service evolving into community service learning comes from Becker College in Worcester, Massachusetts. Although born of a tragedy, the "Be Like Brit" charity has inspired an international partnership among the charitable foundation, Becker College, and the community in Haiti, which was devastated by the January 2010 earthquake. Begun as a service learning opportunity, Becker College students visited Haiti to assist in building an orphanage dedicated to the memory of Britney Gengel, who lost her life in the earthquake while on a college mission trip to Haiti and whose father is a Becker alumnus (Gengel and Gengel 2013). Supported by at least one trip annually, Becker College remains connected to this international site with a global experience that lends itself to a multitude of academic opportunities across disciplines, indeed turning community service into CSL. This Becker College connection to Haiti is an example of what transformational learning opportunities (TLOs) are all about. Growing in popularity among colleges and universities, a TLO can be part of a study abroad course and involve an international internship that has the potential to expand a student's personal development as well as his or her learning (Batey and Lupi 2012).

It should be noted that not all college-community partnerships need to wait until students are admitted to the higher education institution; some of these partnerships can begin prior to students' admission to focus on building readiness for college. One example of a successful college-high school partnership is a project carried out in a relatively small Massachusetts community where high school administrators recognized that not as many students were attending college as they believed were capable of doing so. Working directly with college administrators, they developed an "Early College" program that specifically targeted the middle quartiles of the class, those students achieving satisfactory grades and passing competency exams but likely to be in noncredit, remedial classes if accepted to college (Leonard 2013). In addressing the issue of college readiness, many high schools offer Advanced Placement (AP) courses and dual enrollment programs that partner the high school with the postsecondary education institution. However, what set this Massachusetts example of "Early College" apart was the direct involvement of both high school and college faculty, the establishment of a strong parental support component, and the inclusion of student voice/choice as well. Through the collaboration of all these stakeholders, considerable attention was given to curriculum alignment and increased orientation experiences for students via more visits to the college. Parental support, both emotional and financial, was a key component, as there were costs associated with student participation in the "Early College" program, even though it was subsidized by a local educational foundation (Leonard 2013).

Beyond the secondary school-college partnerships and the practical, often exciting experiences that fieldwork can provide, there are many opportunities within the regular classroom setting for professors to apply twenty-first century skills that would create links to both the local community and the wider world to make a course or class more relevant for today's students. Speaking specifically to teacher education programs, Batey and Lupi (2012) cite Cushner and Mahon (2002) and Villegas and Lucas (2002) in suggesting that an international field-based experience can provide American preservice teachers with a greater understanding of both cultural similarities and differences among peoples of the world. The authors contend that an international experience will better prepare these student teachers for the diversity they will encounter, particularly in urban classrooms throughout the United States (Batey and Lupi 2012). Given that this field-based learning involves first-hand experiences, it can be more transformative than anything provided within the traditional classroom setting.

International programs do represent major endeavors by colleges and universities, but they are not absolutely necessary for an institution to provide transformative learning opportunities. Essentially, it is possible to provide such experiences on a much smaller scale. The essential component of a TLO is giving students the chance to connect with the community while incorporating many twenty-first century skills and literally transforming students' thinking. One example is an undergraduate writing class at Goodwin College in East Hartford, Connecticut, where the professor asks each student to identify an area of expertise that then becomes the topic for blog posts the student will write. This specialized connection to community and the wider world serves a dual purpose of developing writing skills and using technology in a real-world context. "The blog becomes an opportunity for students to develop brand identities for themselves that both distinguish their voices and their perspectives as unique, while simultaneously situating themselves within the constellation of similar blogs maintained by other students and writers across the globe" (Laist 2013, 14).

The Role of Technology

As seen in the previous example, links to community are not the only types of connections that need to be an integral part of the modern college or university classroom. The use of technology affords students the opportunity to connect in multiple ways to resources of all types that can provide information about a limitless number of topics, institutions, and organizations around the world as well as experts representing all possible fields of study. One innovative use of technology is the addition of experiential learning simulations to the instructional repertoire of professors, making real-life connections possible while supporting a student-centered approach.

Through a partnership with a local technology firm called Toolwire, undergraduate business students at State University of New York successfully piloted a Digital Media Simulation episode that was self-paced and asynchronous, demonstrating that this new technology could increase student engagement while fostering deep learning (Beckem and Watkins 2012). This particular simulation was designed "to keep learners focused on essential course objectives ... [moving] beyond current methodologies to embody what might best be described as enhanced, authentic assessments" (Beckem and Watkins 2012, 63). Beckem and Watkins (2012) also indicated that another advantage of the power of Digital Media Simulation was its ease of use for instructors as well as both the reliability and scalability of the product. Again, the college connection to the business community helped to make this experiential learning opportunity possible and successful.

Another way that technology connections can occur seamlessly in the classroom is through a "flipped" model, adding again to student engagement and diminishing the nagging issue of the level of students' preparedness for class. The flipped classroom model is one that stimulates student involvement in the lesson prior to coming to class, again shifting the focus away from the instructor as knowledge provider and more toward a learner-centered approach that actively engages the student in course content and concepts (Berrett 2012). Student involvement prior to an actual class session often entails use of the Internet to research real-world applications of a topic or seek different perspectives that are shared later through collaborative in-class activities. This approach represents another way college-level classes can connect today's students to the wider global community to enhance authentic learning.

Potential Drawbacks

Although there are many benefits associated with making the classroom a place where multiple connections link higher education to the community, one potential drawback to including these types of courses and programs must be mentioned. Some within academia who offer innovative classes, courses, and programs are concerned that their institutional evaluations as professors may potentially be compromised because of the nature of these instructional methods. The Community-Campus Partnerships for Health (CCPH), a national organization that promotes health equity and social justice by creating partnerships between institutions of higher education and the community, contends that this concern may be pertinent to some professors involved in these types of courses and programs. Specifically, CCPH raises the issue that standards for promotion or tenure at colleges and universities usually reflect a traditional approach to meeting these stated requirements; in turn, these promotion/tenure requirements may act as barriers for those professors whose classes and courses involve innovative community partnerships (Seifer, Blanchard, Jordan, Gelmon, and McGinley 2012). For example, one component often evaluated is the requirement for scholarly writing; the publication of peer-reviewed journal articles is a typical criterion used to demonstrate scholarship for promotion. However, writing about community-based scholarship may not lend itself as easily to traditional scholarly journals (Seifer et al. 2012). As community-based learning and research become more common and a more integral part of the collegiate approach to twenty-first century learning, this legitimate issue may be one that college professors will want to explore further with higher education administrators.

Finally, it is necessary to address a fundamental question: as professors become more inspired to connect to their communities and the real world, are they ready for all that this major transition will entail? In striving to meet the needs of a new generation of scholars—scholars who are also "doers"—a similar question is posed by a group of professors at Wilfrid Laurier University in Canada (Curwood, Munger, Mitchell, Mackeigan, and Farrar 2011): are the colleges and universities ready to make this shift in focus? Citing Ostrander (2004), these professors (Curwood et al. 2011) point out that greater interest in links among higher education, democracy, and civic engagement has led to increased interest in community service learning. They define CSL as the integration of community with intentional learning activities that "ground academia in 'real-world' knowledge and actively contribute to the improvement of local and national social conditions" (Curwood et al. 2011, 15).

Curwood et al. (2011) also speak to the level of cooperation necessary for effective partnerships and stress the importance of the college or university assessing readiness prior to initiating any collaborative CSL or CRB programs. Identifying three key areas, the authors raise specific questions about the commitment levels of the institution, department, and individual faculty members; the resources available to the partnership, including funding and necessary space; and the status of the infrastructure that should be in place for data management. They also caution that planning for direct lines of communication prior to implementing any partnership project is essential for success (Curwood et al. 2011). These suggestions represent appropriate advice for institutions of higher education planning to increase their college-community connections.

Conclusion

Connecting college and community expresses one of the best ways for the professoriate to ensure that their students' college experience is both relevant and representative of twenty-first century skills in action. College is more than learning for learning's sake. Given the rising cost of a college education, college is increasingly about preparing adult learners for a future that is difficult to forecast, particularly in terms of employment. One important aspect of that preparation is gaining real-world experience where students have an opportunity to apply in meaningful ways the skills and knowledge learned in the classroom. This learning can happen best when higher education institutions connect and utilize the resources available within both their local communities as well as the global community. For the professoriate, recognizing a new paradigm in which college courses and programs are connected to the local, national, and international community through relationships that are mutually supportive and interdependent is essential. If the professoriate seeks relevancy within the curriculum through these community connections, ultimately this approach will benefit students and make progress within academia in moving toward achieving its twenty-first century goals.

Points to Remember

- The professoriate of the twenty-first century must take higher education students beyond the classroom walls, focusing on relevancy as provided by the real-world applications of the skills and knowledge students acquire across the disciplines.

- Multiple opportunities exist for college students in local, national, and international settings for fieldwork, which is an essential part of a postsecondary education in a global society. Many of these experiences may also have an element of community service learning, fostering humanitarian considerations and helping students to develop greater empathy.

- It is the responsibility of the modern professoriate to take advantage of opportunities for collaboration between the college/university and the community, incorporating these experiences into the curriculum across the disciplines to provide students with highly relevant learning situations.

References

Batey, J. J., and M.H. Lupi. 2012. Reflections on student interns, cultural awareness developed through a short-term international internship. *Teacher Education Quarterly* 39(3): 25–44.

Beckem, J. M., and M. Watkins. 2012. Bringing life to learning: Immersive experiential learning simulations for online and blended courses. *Journal of Asynchronous Learning Networks* 16(5):61–71.

Berrett, D. 2012, February 19. How "flipping" the classroom can improve the traditional lecture. *The Chronicle of Higher Education.* Retrieved from http://chronicle.com/article/How-Flipping-the-Classroom/130857/

Bush, G. W. 2016. Points of light. Retrieved from http://www.pointsoflight.org/about-us

Curwood, S. E., F. Munger, T. Mitchell, M. Mackeigan, and A. Farrar. 2011. Building Effective community-university partnerships: Are universities truly ready? *Michigan Journal of Community Service Learning* 17(2):15–26.

Cushner, K., and J. Mahon. 2002. Overseas student teaching: Affecting personal, professional, and global competencies in an age of globalization. *Journal of Studies in International Education* 6(1): 44–58.

Daggett, W. R. 2008. *Rigor and relevance from concept to reality.* Rexford, NY: International Center for Leadership in Education.

Friedman, T. L., and M. Mandelbaum. 2011. *That used to be us: How America fell behind in the world it invented and how we can come back.* New York: Farrar, Straus, and Giroux.

Gengel, L., and C. Gengel, G. with Brozek. 2013. *Heartache and hope in Haiti.* Deerfield Beach, FL: TriMark Press.

Jensen, E. 2009. *Teaching with poverty in mind.* Alexandria, VA: Association for Supervision and Curriculum Development.

Kereluik, K., P. Mishra, C. Fahnoe, and L. Terry. 2013. What knowledge is of most worth: Teacher knowledge for 21st century learning. *Journal of Digital Learning in Teacher Education* 29(4):127–140.

Laist, R. 2013. What can evolutionary psychology teach us about pedagogy? *New England Faculty Development Consortium Exchange* 26(6):11–14.

Latham, D., M. Gross, and S. Witte. 2013. Preparing teachers and librarians to collaborate to teach 21st century skills: Views of LIS and education faculty. *School Library Research Journal* 16:1–23.

Latham, G. 2013. The responsive reading teacher. *Australian Journal of Teacher Education* 38(8):62–72.

Leonard, J. 2013. Maximizing college readiness for all through parental support. *School Community Journal* 23(1):183–202.

McFarlane, D. A. 2011. Multiple intelligences: The most effective platform for global 21st century educational and instructional methodologies. *College Quarterly* 14(1):1–8.

National Council of Teachers of English. 2013. Retrieved from http://www.ncte.org/gover nance/21stcenturyframework

Ostrander, S. A. 2004. Democracy, civic participation, and the university: A comparative study of civic engagement on five campuses. *Nonprofit and Voluntary Sector Quarterly* 33(1):74–93.

Pink, D. H. 2006. *A whole new mind.* New York: Riverhead Books.

Profile of the American Freshman. 2012, April. *Educational Leadership: College, Careers, Citizenship* 69(7):8.

Seifer, S. D., L.W. Blanchard, C. Jordan, S. Gelmon, and P. McGinley. 2012. Faculty for the engaged campus: Advancing community-engaged careers in the academy. *Journal of Higher Education Outreach and Engagement, 16*(1), 5–20.

Skinner, E. A. 2010. Project Nueva Generación and Grow Your Own teachers: Transforming schools and teachers from the inside out. *Teachers Education Quarterly* Summer: 155-167.

Tyack, D., and L. Cuban. 1995. *Tinkering around utopia: A century of public school reform.* Cambridge, MA: Harvard University Press.

Villegas, A. M., and T. Lucas. 2002. Preparing culturally responsive teachers: Rethinking the curriculum. *Journal of Teacher Education* 53(1):20–32.

Wagner, T. 2012. Calling all innovators. *Educational Leadership* 69(7):66–69.

CHAPTER 8

Academic Identity

The Changing Landscape of the Professoriate

By Rick Roque

Introduction

Several factors are currently forcing an evolution in the structure and systems of American higher education, including technology; shifting student demographics; rapidly changing economic conditions; and the impact of content, structure, and delivery of coursework. It is because of these factors that higher education must evolve; without the adoption of dramatic changes, the stability and viability of postsecondary institutions are increasingly called into question. Thus, higher education administrators must revisit each institution's mission, scope, and faculty preparation to better support the evolving needs of students and the industry (Wulff and Austin 2004).

The Industrial Revolution (circa 1820s–1870s) and the Information Age beginning in the 1960s changed the classical model of higher education and, therefore, the professoriate. The academy revolved around a more liberal and classical goal of education with an emphasis upon the university ideal and its relationship to the broader needs of society (Bowen and Schuster 1986). During this time, the university mission of teaching, research, and community service gradually grew narrower to support the growing economic and industrial needs of society. The shift in higher educational goals placed an increased burden upon the professoriate.

These rapid changes and the conflicting forces within the academy inspire pressures and tensions between faculty, staff, administrators, students, and professors as well as the relationship between academic institutions and private industry as a whole. Furthermore, the life and leadership of the professoriate is increasingly challenged by internal and external forces in higher education (Lindsey 2007). The general decline in enrollment, dwindling government support, and other shifts in student retention and demographics dramatically impact the professoriate and effectiveness within the classroom (Bowen and Schuster 1986). The traditional academic formation at the doctoral level has ill prepared a generation of professors because such programs did not take into account present-day changes. Fluctuations in the labor markets and various industrial sectors have forced the academic market to likewise evolve in support of greater student achievement and success.

Technology is the key driver in the changes in the labor markets, which is motivating the need for the "modern student" to return to higher educational schooling for advanced learning. In addition, the demand of adult workers for online learning via the Internet has grown significantly (Dede 2005). The place, means of delivery, and method of instruction are dynamics placing tremendous strain on American higher educational systems as they strive to serve this vast market and educational need (Szybinski and Jordan 2010). Also, the demands of the public and private markets have contributed to academic changes that have led to a reduction in full-time faculty positions and an increase in part-time adjunct professors who are sometimes inadequately prepared to address the needs of the modern student (Lemmer 2012). Therefore, it is necessary to seriously look at recruiting, retaining, and developing competent faculty members and to re-examine the roles that government, community, and private industry have with higher education (Dede 2005).

The Changing Culture in the Professoriate

Today, higher education relates more closely to the larger economic purposes of American society. These modern changes have often conflicted with the traditional norms within the academic profession and how they have operated historically. Financial constraints and the rapidly changing technological environment have forced the professoriate to work smarter and with greater emphasis on classroom effectiveness than in the past (Lemmer 2012). Faculty careers, the use of adjunct professors, and the shift toward more practical research goals have forced the professoriate to work more collaboratively with community members, students, and other colleagues in academia (Rice 1996). The culture of the professoriate is changing in dramatic ways, growing demographically older and more diverse, with new professors entering educational leadership roles from already successful careers in private industry, scholarly research, or educational administration (Tresey 2007). In this way, the face of the professoriate is evolving into a rich resource for contemporary universities and colleges.

The makeup of the professoriate is not the only change; the actual role of the professoriate within the classroom has also changed. The professoriate has evolved from strict educational management within the classroom to educational leadership principles that inspire a more creative learning process (Dede 2005). In addition, the public, students, administrators, and even professors themselves expect much more of the professoriate. Professors undergo much greater levels of scrutiny to produce and publish meaningful contributions both to academia and to private industry as ways of expanding an institution's influence. These pressures can make the professoriate significantly challenging, more than ever before in the history of the academy (Lemmer 2012). The instructor is expected to master new and changing skills and gain full entry into the academic and industrial world. In today's non-tenured and adjunct atmosphere, it may mean spending several years as a "gypsy scholar," so to speak, moving from university to university in class-by-class appointments simply to gain academic credentials (Boyer 1990). Expectations to publish and contribute to academia conflict with the realities of teaching and administrative service responsibilities, and as a result, the professoriate may sometimes be lonely, stressful, unfocused, and unfulfilling (Tresey 2007).

Welcome to the Lonely World of the Professoriate

In today's professoriate, personal and family needs often compete with professional or academic obligations. This conflict is especially visible when postdoctoral efforts are extended or additional formal academic work is assumed and becomes increasingly common. Exacerbating the lonely realities of the profession is the lack of an established community. The absence of diversity and the marked age gap between first-year and seasoned professors sometimes contribute to this cultural fracture within faculty ranks. An aging faculty reflects past hiring patterns, low turnover rates, and retirement decisions. A relatively large number of professors were hired in the 1960s and 1970s; they are presently retiring, but the exit rates are relatively low because of the economic conditions, thus producing an "aging professoriate" (Clark and Ma 2005). The emerging millennial professoriate clashes with the institutional professors who choose not to retire or who simply cannot afford to retire. This places both a cultural and an economic strain on institutions desiring to evolve more quickly to changes in societal expectations, technological advances, and global economic and market pressures, which are more in tune with the skills and abilities of younger professors. Given these factors, coupled with the lack of collegiality, support systems to guide and mentor first-year professors are frequently either deficient or entirely nonexistent (Dede 2005).

Faculty members describe their initiation period as a time of avoidance, distress, and unproductive beginning (Tresey 2007). There is a Darwinistic component to faculty dynamics as newer faculty members are introduced to tenured or more senior faculty members within an institution. The new faculty experience can weigh heavily upon novice professors because significant anxiety revolves around keeping their jobs from class-to-class, semester-to-semester (Murray 2008). The lack of time to balance the demands of classroom preparation and research adds to this stress. The time to learn new pedagogical strategies and focus on scholarly research is replaced with increased course work and elevated administrative responsibilities resulting from department budget cuts. Where is the time to revise curricula, write grant proposals, and keep up with new trends within a respective field? Given the current economic pressures, institutions of higher education across the country continue to impose more demands on faculty. As they continue to cut back on resources, colleges and universities expect far more from their faculty members (Szybinski and Jordan 2010). Consequently, providing support for faculty development is more critical than ever.

Between balancing personal and professional needs as well as completing the necessary preparatory requirements for each class, the professoriate struggles to meet these growing demands (Boyer 1990). Support from senior faculty members is most beneficial; however, given the dynamics mentioned earlier, it is frequently lacking. In the modern professoriate, faculty members often do not spend enough time with senior colleagues, which undercuts the collegial atmosphere in each respective department. Building a sense of community is vital for the overall success of the professoriate because it offers the opportunity for professors to share research, without which new ideas generated from faculty collaboration are undermined. New ideas exchanged through collaborative research, and the resulting collegial culture, are essential to the growth and sustenance of the professoriate (Murray 2008).

The Millennial Contribution to the Professoriate

The change in faculty demographics mirrors the diversity in the student body, and therefore, the financial dependencies have also changed. With the growing trend to integrate the student experience within real-world settings, greater investments in these emerging educational technologies are necessary to match the learning styles of millennials (Tresey 2007). As a result, the delivery and business models for American higher education have changed, and the professoriate is pivotal in successfully facilitating this shift. Millennials are more diverse, technologically savvy, and globally aware than any other previous generation (Howe and Strauss 2007). Emerging learning styles contribute to students collaborating in learning communities, leveraging multiple media tools, and studying in varied remote environments (Dede 2005). As a result, trends that support and enhance collaboration among peers both professionally and interpersonally are central to their college-level learning experience.

Faculty engagement is changing, and pressures are being placed on more traditional, managerial styles of administrative or classroom governance as more millennials become personnel in key administrative and professoriate positions. For millenials, the philosophy of education and administrative management revolves around collaboration and is largely more democratic at its core (Howe and Strauss 2007). As millennials enter and eventually dominate the first-year professoriate, friction with older, more experienced professors and those within the administrative ranks will almost certainly increase. Lastly, because millennials are more diverse, they are accustomed to engaging with people from various social, ethnic, linguistic, and racial perspectives. As a result, classroom pedagogy today is far more diverse, explorative, and engaging when compared to the lecture-based model that has historically dominated American higher educational structures (Dede 2005). This pedagogical evolution will undoubtedly continue.

The millennial generation is driving profound change in higher education, and there is no other place where this change is more visible than in the classroom (Szybinski and Jordan 2010). Access to information is commoditized, as it is freely accessible on the Internet. Because this development has dramatically changed the student learning process, how the professoriate engages with students must necessarily change with it. Social trends particular to millennials require the modern classroom to support and encourage opportunities for collaboration, visualization of content, rapid digestion of details in shorter time intervals, and more deeply personal student expression (Howe and Strauss 2007). To accomplish all this and ensure that new instructional strategies are used effectively in the classroom, staff professional development opportunities are essential.

The initial and ongoing development of the professoriate should emulate the very strategies that are intended to be used in the classroom, thus requiring an overhaul in existing staff development and curriculum planning efforts as well as the application of next-generation training for the professoriate within doctoral programs across the United States. There is a significant need to provide ongoing professional development for faculty members at all career levels and all ranks, including adjunct professors, through mentoring, collaboration, and training in new pedagogical methods and technologies (Szybinski and Jordan 2010). Such efforts will also foster a more collegial culture among new professors and senior faculty and administrators.

Opportunities Moving Forward: Diversity and Development

Clear lessons and opportunities to support the professoriate can only be developed with a thorough understanding of the challenges and their underlying factors. Diversity, generational factors, and mentoring are important forces within American higher education, and they should be adequately understood so that the experience and quality of the professoriate can be improved. The evolution of higher education is shaped by changes in the demographics of entering students and faculty members alike. Thus, new methods of teaching and learning are required. There has been a distinct evolution of the professoriate to support these recent shifts in the knowledge that society values. Accelerated advances in information technology introduce opportunities for professional development for all staff, but especially for those with many years in the professoriate.

Younger members of the professoriate are more familiar with these recent changes, which can cause a distinct rift among faculty members, particularly with older, more senior colleagues (Murray 2008). This rift within the professoriate is often worsened by evolving disparities in age, diversity, and the perceived need for part-time scholars and full-time practitioners. However, such rifts can be corrected with the appropriate administrative leadership and collegial focus to establish generational ties across faculty ranks. Millenials are the most diverse generation in the history of civilized societies (Ehrenberg 2010), and this unique student diversity yields considerable benefits by elevating dialogue and presenting opportunities for deeper collaboration among faculty members and across institutions. With increasingly diverse classrooms, the professoriate at any given institution of higher education should mirror these trends.

At a time of intense the polarization in politics and significant economic, religious, and social differences in the culture, diversity in age, gender, religion, and race on a college or university campus fulfills an institutional responsibility to students and the surrounding communities (Szybinski and Jordan 2010). Millennials have an organic technological and social awareness of the benefits of diversity; it is central to who they are, how they have educationally evolved, and how they run industry (Howe and Strauss 2007). Postsecondary institutions can take advantage of the opportunities to increase higher education access for immigrants and members of other underrepresented communities as well as to encourage a career direction that would include the professoriate. With a diverse and relatable faculty, the professoriate can assume a much-needed position within the classroom and the community as role models and mentors to students and one another.

The Keys to Success in the Professoriate

There are many challenges to the professoriate, but given the evolving nature of society, its growing diversity, and the technological and social advances inherent in the millennial generation, there are also many opportunities for an institution to foster the best performing academic environment and culture possible. To do so, there are several adjustments an institution of higher education can explore to keep up with the rapid pace of change—both the internal change within the organization and the external change of contemporary competitive pressures.

Federal law altered human resource practices outlawing mandatory retirement policies. Retirement practices and the tenure system should be revisited to refresh faculty hiring and to avoid burdensome labor and health care costs. Institutions should respond more proactively to the changing industrial and economic needs of society, and options to promote early retirement will create opportunities for up-and-coming professors in an increasingly competitive market (Ehrenberg 2010). With a more dynamic and free-flowing faculty, the need to define and align the strategic plan arises. Understanding the future needs for hiring new faculty, completing adequate university planning, offering faculty retreats and other department building opportunities, and fostering an open environment that challenges the status quo and is receptive to new ideas to better support professors and students are all vital activities to foster an increasingly diverse faculty. Too often, budget constraints, lack of time, and a resistant culture undermine the collegial opportunities within the professoriate (Dede 2005). The ultimate objective is to openly and safely discuss new ideas that may produce better results, be more cost-effective, and yield a higher rate of graduates in their respective fields.

While the adjunct, or part-time, professorship expands, it is increasingly important to invest in developing more effective teaching strategies across the professoriate for both full-time and adjunct faculty members. This sort of systemic professional development will not only establish a deeper and more collegial faculty, but it will also build a broader bridge between full-time and adjunct professors. Such an effort will better facilitate the changing dynamics within the professoriate and more uniformly improve the student experience. Adjunct professors are commonly hired "off the street" and given a classroom to teach a subject without any previous teaching experience. This practice divides the ranks within the professoriate. Classroom instructional strategies, better use of technology, and innovative applications of a field of study are all opportunities that could improve with deeper levels of collaboration among faculty members (Lemmer 2012).

Conclusion

Higher education in the United States is undergoing a renaissance in which the very structure and nature of the professoriate is being reexamined. The rapid pace of change, largely driven by technology and the connected sociological factors associated with the millennial generation, are forcing institutions of higher learning to adjust and adapt by implementing changes in hiring practices, employment benefits, and classroom pedagogies. These dynamics are dramatically impacting faculty and staff culture as well as how an institution strategically plans for its future contribution to students and society. The growing appetite for higher-quality postsecondary education is directly connected to the changing landscape of the professoriate, and this market factor will continue to be instrumental in driving future evolution within higher education.

Points to Remember

- Challenges in the professoriate are historically rooted in teaching practices and faculty culture.
- The rapid pace of change associated with the social and technological advances of the millennial generation is driving much of the evolution associated with the shifting landscape of the professoriate.
- The need to embrace more diverse hiring practices is fundamental to the next-generation professoriate.
- The evolving tenure system needs revising to refresh faculty hiring practices and to restructure retirement packages to better align with the financial goals of an institution and its longer-term commitment to staff.
- Strategic planning for faculty is necessary to align institutional planning and the future needs of faculty. The planning efforts need to be outcome based, measurable, and the result of open and free discussions fostered during the planning sessions.
- Investing in next-generation pedagogy is needed for the professional development of more senior faculty and staff members, who must take advantage of new trends, technologies, and practices that lead to a better functioning organization with anticipated improved student outcomes.
- Innovation in teaching is important and can be accomplished in several ways. It may include specific pedagogical practices to inspire a more innovative and creative culture within the classroom, but it may also mean innovation in hiring practices in the people who are hired. Finding candidates from nontraditional sources to fill vacancies can lead to more innovative outcomes if they feel authentically welcomed as part of the broader faculty and staff and if they believe that their contribution is factored into overall planning efforts.

References

Bowen, H., and J. Schuster. 1986. *American professors: A national resource imperiled.* Fair Lawn, NJ: Oxford University Press.

Boyer, E. 1990. *Scholarship reconsidered: Priorities of the professoriate.* Lawrenceville, NJ: Princeton University Press.

Clark, R., and J. Ma. 2005. *Recruitment, retention, and retirement in higher education.* North-ampton, MA: Edward Elgar.

Dede, C. 2005. *Planning for neomillennial learning styles: Implications for investments in technology and faculty.* Louisville, CO: EDUCAUSE.

Ehrenberg, R. G. 2010, June. *Rethinking the professoriate.* Ithaca, NY: Cornell Higher Educa-tion Research Institute, Cornell University. Retrieved from http://digitalcommons.ilr.cornell.edu/ workingpapers/117/

Howe, N., and W. Strauss. 2007, July–August. The next 20 years: How customer and workforce attitudes will evolve. *Harvard Business Review* 85(7–8):41–52.

Lemmer, E. M. 2012. Sustaining the academic self: Challenges to the professoriate in a changing higher education landscape. *Journal for Christian Scholarship* 48(1–2):1–25.

Lindsey, M. 2007, January 11. *The challenges and opportunities of transitioning from PhD student to junior faculty.* Presentation given at the 12th annual meeting of the Society for Social Work Research, San Francisco. Retrieved from http://www.slideserve.com/kaia/the-challenges-opportunities-of-transitioning-from-phd-student-to-junior-faculty

Murray, J. 2008. New faculty members' perceptions of the academic work life. *Journal of Human Behavior in the Social Environment* 17(1–2):107–128.

Rice, E. 1996. *Making a place for the new American scholar.* New Pathways: Faculty Career and Employment for the 21st Century Working Paper Series, Inquiry No. 1. Washington, DC: American Association for Higher Education.

Szybinski, D., and T. Jordan. 2010, Summer. Navigating the future of the professoriate. *Peer Review* 12(3):4–6.

Tresey, P. S. 2007, Spring. Experiences of educational leadership faculty in the first year of the professoriate: A phenomenological study (Paper No. 296). *Electronic Theses and Dis-sertations.* Retrieved from http://digitalcommons.georgiasouthern.edu/etd

Wulff, D., and A. Austin. 2004. *Paths to the professoriate: Strategies for enriching the preparation of future faculty.* San Francisco: Jossey-Bass.

CHAPTER 9

The Fundamentals of Virtual Teaching

Opportunities and Approaches

By Nicholas D. Young and Elizabeth Jean

Throughout their own postsecondary education experience, professors were taught how to work face-to-face with students in meaningful ways. The traditional brick-and-mortar classroom provided professors easy access to communicate and connect with students on topics related to specific course content. Assignments, projects, and discourse all happened within the natural workings of the classroom structure. Limitations were set by the classroom walls and the specific time frame of the class (Young and Celli 2013).

In the traditional classroom, professors would lecture, students would take notes, conversations would ensue, and at the end of class, professors would give the assignment for the next class. The process would repeat itself each week, sometimes two or three times a week. Students would seek out materials from the library, and at times it would take several weeks for books or articles to arrive from another library or location. At the end of the course, there was usually a culminating event, exam, or paper due.

Fast-forward to the new and exciting world of online learning. "Still in its infancy at just twenty years old, online education offers infinite possibilities and configurations" (Hill 2012, 85). Brick-and-mortar limitations are practically extinct, as professors can connect and communicate with students in a multitude of ways regardless of location or time of day. The trick is to make sure those connections and conversations further academic discourse, improve learning, and offer experiences to students that were not possible prior to the dawn of virtual education.

It is not enough for the professor to post the readings and assignments on a website and receive the required assignments in return. This flat learning will not create the discourse or connection that is vital to educational growth and understanding. A professor truly wishing to leverage the virtual world and use it to the benefit of students will seek out, learn, and internalize best practices for virtual learning. The question then becomes, what do professors need to know to teach online in a way that is creative and furthers academics in a meaningful way?

Who Are Virtual Learners?

Understanding the demographics of virtual learners is key to acknowledging the new breed of learner and the intricacies that make these students so different from face-to-face learners. Noel-Levitz explains that "satisfied learners are more likely to be successful students" and, thus, more likely to graduate (2012, 2). The *2013 National Online Learners Priorities Report* analyzed more than 114,000 students over a three-year time span from the fall of 2010 through the spring of 2013 at 104 institutions (Noel-Levitz 2013). Of these students, almost 106,000 were exclusively online learners, and approximately 5,900 attended classes on a college campus, with the remaining students undeclared in enrollment status (Noel-Levitz 2013, 4). In comparison, the 2012 report showed that of the 123,500 students from 109 institutions questioned, 112,000 of them declared themselves as primarily online learners, while 10,000 students were enrolled on campus (Noel-Levitz 2012, 4). While the 2013 report shows a slightly smaller sampling, the findings clearly shows the continued use of virtual programming for educational advancement.

According to the *National Online Learners Priorities Report* (Noel-Levitz 2013, 5), 70% of the participating students were female, and most were Caucasian. The age demographic revealed equal percentages (29%) in the 25–34 age bracket and 35–44 age bracket, 23% in the 45–54 age bracket, with the remaining 19% bookending the age span with the under 24 age bracket and the over 55 age bracket (Noel-Levitz 2013, 5). Of the over 114,000 enrolled students questioned, 95% took primarily online classes, while the remaining 5% preferred brick-and-mortar classes (Noel-Levitz 2013, 5). In addition, most learners worked full time while pursuing their degree, and half of the students questioned owned their own home (Noel-Levitz 2013, 5).

Lastly, Noel-Levitz examined at the class level as a demographic comparison. Overall, the virtual student demographic showed 73,000 undergraduates and 36,000 graduate students, with the remaining student population undeclared (2013, 4). The graduate-level learner came in at 32% with the majority share; the report continued with dropping percentages for the first-, second-, third-, and fourth-year learners with percentages of 28, 17, 14, and 11, respectively (Noel-Levitz 2013, 5). It is interesting to note that 44% of the population questioned "have a graduate-level goal of obtaining a doctorate or master's degree" (Noel-Levitz 2013, 5).

Virtual learners seem driven to improve their role in the global economy; working while taking classes is the norm rather than the exception. Professors must understand and cater to this type of learner. The virtual academic spectrum includes a plethora of delivery models to suit the needs of various learners and those of the course content.

Delivery Models

The World Wide Web has opened the floodgates to virtual education. There are various class types ranging from blended/hybrid to fully online, from classes taught by instructors to classes that are self-taught. This "virtual tsunami" (Brooks 2012) has created educational opportunities for all sorts of learners. What follows is a description of the most common virtual delivery models.

Blended/hybrid. The blended or hybrid delivery model combines "the best elements of online and face-to-face education" (Watson 2008, 3). At its best, blended learning provides online opportunities to learn educational content while retaining the most important features of the traditional classroom, such as personalized interactions and thoughtful discourse. The most important aspect of blended learning may be "the shift in instructional strategy" (Watson 2008, 5). The flipped classroom is an example of this shift.

In the flipped classroom, instructional pods are taught via the Internet during noncontact hours. Classroom time is then used to apply the concepts learned, further the discussion, and review questions. Put another way, the "common theme is to make face-to-face class time more effective, using it to provide much of the instructor feedback and interactive skills portion of a class while pushing content delivery into more efficient online tools" (Hill 2012, 92).

This enhanced classroom learning experience allows students to spend their face-to-face time solving problems, digging deeper, and sharing experiences. It effectively buys the professor time to address student problems on an individual or small group basis. Perhaps the best definition of a blended classroom is this: "Teachers approach their role differently, as guides and mentors instead of purveyors of information, [and] classrooms must be redefined as flexible learning environments" (Watson 2008, 16).

100% Virtual. The 100% virtual course is just that—100% online. There is no face-to-face interaction, no brick-and-mortar location. Students and professors can access it from anywhere at anytime. Assignments are completed online, papers are uploaded by the student to the professor, comments and grades are also returned online. Contact is made via e-mail, social media, internal postings, or blogs.

Pelletier suggests that there are four need-to-know items for online professors to remember:

- Presence: Online learning requires a professor to be exceptionally dedicated. While a 100% virtual course is more convenient, it is also more time consuming.
- Communication: This is key online. Strong communication often means a professor must reiterate what a student says to ensure clarity of response.
- Discussion: Online discussion is where the "heart of the [virtual] learning happens. ... Exceptional facilitators must have frequent and active presence in the discussion" (2013, 12)
- Constructive Feedback: A rubric is a must, along with both positive and negative feedback.

For some professors, this distant way of teaching and learning is fine, but for others, the criticism looms. Online teaching/learning is less personal and necessitates that both parties be independent in thought and practice. For instructors, face-to face teaching must morph into creative and interesting online curriculum objectives while still maintaining high standards (Bejerano 2008). Online teaching requires the professor to possess an organizational skill set and the ability to structure tasks for students without the benefit of personal interactions.

Instructional Tools: Platforms

The use of an online platform to guide the setup and management of course instruction is commonplace in most institutions of higher education. New platforms are being developed all the time; some are for-profit, such as Blackboard Learning Systems, and some are open-source (i.e., free), such as Moodle. Each has its intricacies, abilities, and pitfalls, but the professor's comfort level with the platform, or learning management system (LMS), will drive online class creativity, instruction, and student learning.

Blackboard Learning Systems. Blackboard offers a virtual classroom with a multitude of options for management, collaboration, and learning. Institutions pay for the ability to design their own virtual courses within the confines of Blackboard's offerings. The Blackboard site touts the ability to "combine our expertise with yours to create a better education experience at your academic institution" (Blackboard, n.d., n.p.). However, some research suggests that it is "the framework that constrains professors from much-needed interactions with students" (Coopman 2009, n.p.)

Blackboard provides a road map to help institutions and professors create online classes. Blackboard's website (n.d.) describes a four-point system meant to be all inclusive:

- Teaching and Learning: Implement a high-performing platform designed to attain institutional goals for teaching and learning.
- Adoption and Expansion: Utilize collaborative solutions meant to meet the needs of a wide group of users, with highest return on investment.
- Administrative Services: Leverage the platform for organizing meetings as well as completing administrative services to adequately meet student needs.
- Release Upgrades: Expand capabilities through platform improvements and system upgrades.

Blackboard's website features testimonials about the experiences of many colleges and universities. Among them, the University of Cincinnati boasts "nearly 4,000 courses with Blackboard-hosted content per semester," which includes approximately two-thirds of the faculty (Blackboard, n.d.). Northern Illinois University was impressed with the toolbox provided by Blackboard, which allowed the university to move many classes toward the flipped classroom model (Blackboard, n.d.).

In addition, Blue Mountain Community College commented on the financial savings associated with Blackboard (n.d.). The significant savings realized by Blue Mountain eventually resulted in the platform's implementation across the 17 community colleges in Oregon (Blackboard, n.d.). Cost-effectiveness is one reason to compare Blackboard to Moodle, a free platform solution with many of the same capabilities and functions.

Moodle (Modular Object Oriented Dynamic Learning Environment). Moodle is an open-source online courseware platform. Moodle's (n.d.) site explains that "the heart of Moodle is courses that contain activities and resources" (n.p.). There are approximately 20 activity types that can be combined into "sequences and groups, which can help … guide participants through learning paths" (Moodle n.d., n.p.). Thus, Moodle is a flexible, customizable system that morphs to suit the specific and unique needs of the college/university or faculty member.

Moodle is especially prevalent in smaller institutions where community development and financial constraints are more noticeable (Straumsheim 2014). Professors or institutions may create a complete virtual classroom. According to a Smith College (n.d.) document entitled *Moodle Basics for Instructors,* the Moodle platform may be helpful for the following tasks:

- Organizing and delivering digital content (e.g., web links, simulations, podcasts, etc.)
- Capitalizing on learning opportunities, such as PowerPoint presentations, lectures, etc., outside of class time
- Encouraging peer-to-peer discourse and interaction abilities via forums or group assignments
- Managing classroom logistics (i.e., making announcements, updating a calendar, grading, reaching out to individual students, etc.)

The Smith College (n.d.) document goes on to explain how to access Moodle and navigate the system. The detailed notes are easy to follow; a professor could easily create his or her own course with custom settings that would engage students in the online learning process.

Instructional Tools: Online Resources

There is a long list of online resources that professors can utilize when creating, maintaining, and teaching a virtual class of any kind. Two such resources are Massive Open Online Courses (MOOCs) and Open Educational Resources (OERs). MOOCs refer to an entire virtual class, while OERs refer to specific resources a professor might use to enhance an online course. The commonality here is that both are either entirely free or available at little cost.

Massive Open Online Courses. Massive Open Online Courses, in their most recent form, exploded in popularity and became a hot commodity in 2012 (Marques and McGuire 2013). The idea was to weave together top instructors with the best online tools. Based on this theory, Coursera and Udacity were born. Of all the MOOCs available at the time, the edX platform was the only nonprofit among them. According to Marques and McGuire, the response to MOOCs was larger than predicted, with "tens of thousands of students signing up for each class" (2013, 4).

MOOCs have two distinguishing factors: assessments and an endpoint. Students enrolled in MOOCs will have regular assessments and an exam or assignment at the end. These may be graded by an instructor or peer or via software. A MOOC will also span a specific time frame, usually between 4–12 weeks (Marques and McGuire 2013).

Traditionally, MOOCs were open access, meaning the "materials [were] in the public domain and [didn't] have copyright restrictions" (Marques and McGuire 2013, 7). Consequently, these materials were free to use and share. Also, it was common to generate student-to-student and student-to-professor connections. Today's MOOCs function in a slightly different way, with much of the material being copyrighted and becoming unavailable when the course ends. Significantly, more recent MOOCs are "less open to interaction among its participants" (Marques and McGuire 2013, 7).

MOOCs are produced by various sources. Udemy, Coursera, and Udacity began as online MOOCs; however, there are also many elite universities now offering MOOCs. The list includes Stanford, UC Berkeley, MIT, Duke, UCLA, Harvard, and Carnegie Mellon, whose site touts "no instructors, no credits, no charge" (Carnegie Mellon University 2015, n.p.). The Yale University Center for Teaching and Learning's (2016) website boasts "free and open access to a selection of introductory courses taught by distinguished teachers and scholars at Yale University. The aim of the project is to expand access to educational materials for all who wish to learn" (n.p.). Their classes are offered on numerous platforms, including Coursera, iTunes, YouTube, and Yale's very own OpenYaleCourse (Yale Center for Teaching and Learning 2016).

With all these variables to contend with, a clear definition of a MOOC might be helpful. Put simply, a MOOC is an educational resource resembling a class, that has assessment mechanisms and an endpoint, provides direct online instruction to an unlimited number of students, and is often taught by the institution's own professors (Lucas 2013; Marques and

McGuire 2013; Young, Jean, and Michael 2015). An evolving online tool, MOOCs are sure to continue to transform academic classes for the masses, and professors will necessarily have to increase efforts to keep in contact with the growing number of students interested in their class content.

Open Educational Resources. Open Educational Resources refer to high-quality resources that provide digital libraries, podcasts, textbooks, lectures, course modules, and games for a myriad of educational applications that are accessible to students, teachers, and the general public and are accessible at little or no cost (Young et al. 2015). In 2002, Hewlett Foundation funded two projects, one through MIT and the other through Carnegie Mellon (Groom 2013). These two programs, more than any others, opened the OER floodgates.

The program at MIT, called OpenCourseWare, is the model for many other colleges and universities worldwide. Its repository holds nearly all the materials produced by MIT for approximately 2,000 courses (EDUCAUSE 2010). Typically, instructors or students will download materials to use within their own class. Online professors will find OERs to be the crux of their program, as pulling from various sites makes the online class more interesting, and the modular nature of each OER allows for a multitude of combinations that the professor can tailor to the specific nature of the class (EDUCAUSE 2010).

Khan Academy is an example of a not-for-profit, noncollege-sponsored OER. Salman Khan has created over 3,500 ten-minute lessons that can be seen on YouTube (Khan Academy n.d.). Its mission is "to provide a free, world-class education for anyone, anywhere" (Khan Academy n.d., n.p.). Content includes lessons in science, mathematics, finance, computer science, and economics. Lessons are broken down into bite-sized pieces, and at the end of the lesson, students can see—among other items—what they spent the most time on. Both professors and parents can access this OER and personalize instruction for students or children.

Social Media

As rapidly as online learning is changing the landscape of post-secondary education, social media is changing online teaching. While there are many examples of social media platforms, interactive concepts such as Facebook, Twitter, and Google Hangouts add asynchronous and synchronous discourse opportunities to classes while offering a host of other teaching applications. YouTube and TED Talks both offer the ability to post, download, and watch relevant video clips. Faculty members should take a deeper look at these and other social media tools to understand how they add to the world of online teaching in terms of their importance for the professor.

Facebook, Twitter, and Blogs. Facebook and Twitter offer a plethora of ways to engage students in online education. Resources are limitless, projects and assignments can be discussed and reviewed, and the sharing of materials and concepts through these social media platforms is second nature for many students (OnlineCollege.org 2012). Facebook and Twitter all allow for collaboration among students and inclusive of professors. The face-to-face time lacking in traditional online classes can be found using these tools to conduct online office hours, host remote speakers, and connect in group chats (2014).

Using Twitter, OnlineCollege.org facilitates a weekly chat for faculty members "focused on topics related to online learning" (Venable and Milligan 2012, 2). This chat session offers professors a chance to understand and practice using both asynchronous and synchronous forms of Twitter to engage students and further discussion. Although Twitter is somewhat limited by its 140-character messages, it is one way that professors can use social media to enhance virtual education.

Blogs provide an additional source of media connection for students and professors. A blog is "a website that contains online personal reflection, comments, and often hyperlinks provided by the writer" (Merriam-Webster, n.d., n.p.). Professors can start their own using a number of different platforms, including Blackboard and Moodle. Among other things, these blogs can direct student learning and offer links to additional resources. Even though the nature of a blog is asynchronous, students can add comments.

YouTube and TED Talks. YouTube and TED Talks offer uploaded videos for use by professors, students, and the general public. Professors can direct students to a particular video clip using the URL address, upload a specific video and attach commentary prior to the students watching the video, or ask the students to find a video that matches the content of the virtual class and post it on the class blog or interactive discussion board with their own commentary. Regardless of the way in which video clips are used, they provide a powerful resource for the online classroom.

According to *PC Magazine* (n.d.), YouTube is the "largest video sharing site on the web" (n.p.). Launched in 2005, YouTube provides content of all kinds, from lectures to funny happenings, from serious educational topics to mundane moments in life. YouTube "connects, informs, and inspires others across the globe and acts as a distribution platform for original content" (YouTube n.d., n.p.). Professors use this distribution platform to find and share video content with their students as a way to inform and expand the learning. Some professors will produce their own channel on YouTube as a means of controlling the content and lectures their students watch.

TED Talks tend to be of a more serious nature. TED is a nonprofit organization "devoted to spreading ideas, usually in the form of short, powerful talks" (TED Conferences n.d., n.p.). TED Talks are meant to inspire others as well as change attitudes and the world. TED, which stands for technology, entertainment, and design, began in 1984 as a one-time conference; however, in 2006, the conference became both an annual event and a phenomenon (TED Conferences n.d.). Professors can use TED Talks as stand-alone virtual features or as part of a discussion or assignment.

Social media is changing constantly. Facebook, Twitter, Google Hangouts, and blogs are only a few of the ways in which professors and students connect online. Using the features of each of these media options may provide rich discussion and opportunities for virtual learning. Likewise, YouTube and TED Talks offer professors creative avenues for lectures that are either delivered by the professor or someone else. As virtual learning expands, so too will the dynamic options for connecting faculty with students online.

Principles of Online Teaching

Online teaching is a new type of academia requiring a new set of teaching tools as dissimilar to brick-and-mortar pedagogy as the computer is to the building itself. It is not enough for a professor to choose a platform and resources, put it together in a pretty package, and ask the student to merely click here and upload there. In addition to the connection the professor makes with the student and the creativity the professor puts forth in designing and delivering the course, there is a host of specific elements the professor must exhibit and practice to teach effectively online.

Lists of best practices for effective online teaching abound (Ben-Naim 2014; Dreon 2013; Faculty Focus 2009; Hanover Research 2009; Pelletier 2013). Listed here is a condensed version of the best practices a professor must consider and apply when teaching a virtual class:

- Be present several times a week or, better yet, with daily check-ins. Respond to e-mails and add to post discussions, blogs, or other social media.
- Create community. Be sure to create an environment where discourse is the norm between student and professor as well as among students.
- Vary the course content between posts, projects, podcasts, videos, or articles. Make it rigorous but attainable.
- Set clear expectations regarding time management, the syllabus, and e-mail response time. This should all be spelled out. The norm is a 24-hour return on e-mails, one week for projects. If the professor will be unavailable during the class for any reason, he or she should let students know to expect a delay in response.
- Vary the groupings by using small group, whole group, and individual work. Be mindful of students who are in differing time zones when planning group work; a team whose members live in Hawaii and Boston will have trouble connecting because of time differences.
- Use both asynchronous and synchronous activities. Sometimes real-time interaction provides opportunities to brainstorm, while an asynchronous event allows participants to think things through before sharing.
- Ask for feedback. Do not wait until the course is over to check in with students. Find out early on what is working and not working. Make changes based on reasonable feedback.
- Prepare all posts, discussions, and reflections in advance. Quality counts! Encourage critical thinking, and support student reflections. Remember that open-ended questions will generate the most conversation.
- A final project or wrap-up session is critical, as this showcases what the students have learned.
- Give constructive feedback and reprimands in private. E-mail concerns and comments to the student directly. Prompt feedback allows for better learning, but think before writing. A professor cannot take back his or her words, and feedback needs to be spot on. If there may be confusion, set up a conference call.

- Faculty must fully understand and be able to use the learning platform; this aids in the versatility of the class, and it shows students that the professor has a vested interest in the course.
- Build each course carefully and completely. Take adequate time to plan, include all necessary aspects, then go back and add additional resources to enhance the class.
- Be flexible but not a pushover—a deadline is a deadline!
- Be respectful of diverse learners by using visual and auditory learning tools as well as written items.

Conclusion

Online teaching is still relatively new, and all things virtual are in constant flux: changing, upgrading, and morphing into better and different ways of educating the twenty-first century postsecondary student. These virtual learners are markedly different from traditional classroom students, and the majority of them see educational goals as a means to career advancement. Brick-and-mortar teaching, while still incredibly valuable, has been greatly influenced by the advent of virtual education, including the blended/hybrid and 100% virtual models; platforms such as Blackboard and Moodle; and resources such as OERs, MOOCs, social media, TED Talks, and YouTube.

In addition to the nuts and bolts of virtual education, social media plays an important role as well, connecting professors and students in meaningful discourse outside of the classroom boundaries. By implementing a long list of suggested practices for professors who wish to engage and support virtual learners in meaningful ways, virtual education can be the best of both worlds: face-to-face and online. It is clear, though, that virtual education has not yet hit its stride, and it may never, with bold new ways of teaching and learning yet to be imagined.

Points to Remember

- Virtual learners are driven to improve their role in the global economy while maintaining other aspects of their life.
- Instructional platforms, such as Moodle, guide the setup and teaching of online courses.

- Massive Open Online Courses (MOOCs), Open Educational Resources (OERs), and other comparable instructional tools create, maintain, and teach all for free or at minimal cost.
- Video sharing and social media are continuously changing and expanding the ways in which professors and students connect.
- A plethora of best practices exists for online teaching, including the following:
  - Be present.
  - Create community.
  - Set clear expectations.
  - Ask for and give constructive feedback.
  - Be flexible.
  - Be respectful of diverse learners.

References

Ben-Naim, D. 2014. Understanding what tools professors actually want: the need for design thinking in higher ed. *Forbes.* Retrieved from http://www.forbes.com/sites/groupthink/2014/08/26/understanding-what-tools-professors-actually-want-the-need-for-design-thinking-in-higher-ed/

Blackboard. n.d.. *About Blackboard.* Retrieved from http://www.blackboard.com/about-us/index.aspxBlackboard n.d. *Blackboard Collaborate.* Retrieved from http://www.blackboard.com/online-collaborative-learning/blackboard-collaborate.aspx.

Brooks, D. 2012, May 3. The campus tsunami. *The New York Times.* Retrieved from http://www.nytimes.com/2012/05/04/opinion/brooks-the-campus-tsunami.html

Carnegie Mellon University. 2015. *Open Learning Initiative.* Retrieved from http://oli.cmu.edu/

Coopman, S. J. 2009, June 1. A critical examination of Blackboard's e-learning environment [Supplemental material]. *First Monday* 14(6). Retrieved from http://firstmonday.org/ojs/index.php/fm/article/view/2434/2202

Dreon, O. 2013, February 25. Applying the seven principles for good practice to the online classroom. *Faculty Focus: Higher Ed Teaching Strategies from Magna Publications.* Retrieved from http://www.facultyfocus.com/articles/online-education/applying-the-seven-principles-for-good-practice-to-the-online-classroom/

EDUCAUSE Learning Initiative. 2010, May 27. Seven things you should know about open educational resources. Retrieved from https://library.educause.edu/resources/2010/5/7-things-you-should-know-about-open-educational-resources

Faculty Focus. 2009. *Ten principles of effective online teaching: Best practices in distance education.* Madison, WI: Magna Publications. Retrieved from http://www.facultyfocus.com/

free-reports/principles-of-effective-online-teaching-best-practices-in-distance-educ ation/

Groom, C. 2013, March 27. *A guide to open educational resources.* Retrieved from http://www. webarchive.org.uk/wayback/archive/20140614151619/http://www.jisc.ac.uk/publications /programmerelated/2013/Openeducationalresources.aspx

Hanover Research. 2009. *Best practices in online teaching strategies.* Retrieved from http://www. hanoverresearch.com

Hill, P. 2012, November/December. Online educational delivery models: A descriptive view. *EDUCAUSE Review* 47(6). Retrieved from http://er.educause.edu/articles/2012/ 11/online-educational-delivery-models—a-descriptive-view

Khan Academy. N.d.. About. *Khan Academy.org.* Retrieved from https://www.khanacademy. org/about

Lucas, H. C., Jr. 2013. MOOCs and online learning. *EDUCAUSE Review* September/October:54–66.

Marques, J., and R. McGuire. 2013, June 7. What is a massive open online course anyway? MN+R attempts a definition. *MOOC News and Reviews.* Retrieved from http://mooc newsandreviews.com/what-is-a-massive-open-online-course-anyway-attempting-defi nition/

Merriam-Webster. N.d. Blog. *Merriam-Webster.com.* Retrieved from http://www.merriam-webster.com/dictionary/blog

Moodle. 2016, November 8. Pedagogy. *Moodle Docs.* Retrieved from https://docs.moodle. org/32/en/Pedagogy

Noel-Levitz. 2012. *2012 national online learners priorities report.* Coralville, IA: Author. Retrieved from https://www.ruffalonl.com/upload/Papers_and_Research/2012/2012_ Online_Leaners_Report.pdf

Noel-Levitz. 2013. *2013 national online learners priorities report.* Coralville, IA: Author. Retrieved from https://www.ruffalonl.com/upload/Papers_and_Research/2013/SSI%20 PSOL_report_0713.pdf

OnlineCollege.org. 2012, May 21. 99 ways you should be using Facebook in your classroom. *OnlineCollege.org.* Retrieved from http://www.onlinecollege.org/2012/05/21/100-ways-you-should-be-using-facebook-in-your-classroom-updated/

PC Magazine. N.d.. Definition of YouTube. *PCMag.com.* Retrieved from http://www. pcmag.com/encyclopedia/term/57119/youtube

Pelletier, P. 2013, September 20. What online teachers need to know. *Faculty Focus: Higher Ed Teaching Strategies from Magna Publications.* Retrieved from http://www.facultyfocus. com/articles/online-education/what-online-teachers-need-to-know/

Smith College. n.d.. Managing a Moodle course. *Moodle Docs.* Retrieved from https://docs. moodle.org/32/en/Managing_a_Moodle_course

Straumsheim, C. 2014, February 13. Moodle for the masses: Moodle tops Blackboard among small colleges, analysis says. *Inside Higher Ed.* Retrieved from https://www. insidehighered.com/news/2014/02/13/moodle-tops-blackboard-among-small-colleges -analysis-says

TED Conferences, LLC. N.d.. Our organization. *TED.com*. Retrieved from http://www.ted.com/about/our-organization

Venable, M. A., and L. Milligan. 2012, March. *Social media in online higher education: Implementing live Twitter chat discussion sessions.* Los Angeles: OnlineCollege.com. Retrieved from http://www.onlinecollege.org/wp-content/uploads/2012/03/OnlineCollege.org-TwitterChat.pdf

Watson, J. 2008. *Blended learning: The convergence of online and face-to-face education.* Promising Practices in Online Learning Series. Vienna, VA: iNACOL. Retrieved from http://www.inacol.org/resource/promising-practices-in-online-learning-blended-learning-the-convergence-of-online-and-face-to-face-education/

Yale Center for Teaching and Learning. 2016. *Online learning.* Yale University. Retrieved from http://ctl.yale.edu/using-technology/online-learning

Young, N., and L. Celli. 2013. *Collapsing educational boundaries from preschool to PhD: Building bridges across the educational spectrum.* Madison, WI: Atwood Publishing.

Young, N., E. Jean, and C. Michael. 2015. Leveraging public-private partnerships to advance opportunities in K–12 technology. In *Educational entrepreneurship: Promoting public-private partnerships for the 21st century*, edited by N. Young and P. Bittel. Lanham, MD: Roman and Littlefield.

YouTube. N.d.. About YouTube. *YouTube.com*. Retrieved from http://www.youtube.com/yt/about/

Index

A

ACT, 29, 31
Affiliation-Based Teaching (ABT), 49, 50, 51, 52, 53, 55, 56, 57, 58, 59, 61
Albertine, 15
Aljohani, 92
Allison, 38
American Association of University Professors (AAUP), 8
American Federation of Teachers (AFT), 22
American Freshman: National Norms, 105
American International College (AIC), 17, 18, 19, 20, 21, 22
Andrade, 67
Au, 38
Aud, 91
Austin, 117

B

Bair, 12, 62
Balfanz, 61
Ballard, 62
Barden, 75, 76, 79, 81, 82
Barefoot, 33
Barnds, 90, 91
Barnett, 65, 66, 68
Batey, 110, 111
Baxter Magolda, 39
Beckem, 107, 112
Becker College, 110
Bean, 29, 41, 62

Bejerano, 130
Ben-Naim, 136
Berrett, 112
Bianco, 91
Blackboard Learning Systems, 130, 131, 135, 138
Blanchard, 113
Bloom's taxonomy, 64
Blue Mountain Community College, 131
Bonetta, 8, 15, 16, 23
Bovee, 55
Bowen, W.G., 94,
Bowen, H., 117, 118
Boyatzis, 77, 82, 83, 84
Boyer, 119, 120
Braxton, 98
Brier, 98
Brooks, 129
Buchanan, 61
Bush, 109

C

Caffarella, 65, 66, 68
Cameron, 69, 70
Carey, 49, 51, 52, 53, 54, 56, 57
Carnegie Mellon University, 67, 107, 133, 134
Carnevale, 87
Carter, 88, 89, 90
Celli, 51, 52, 127
Chicago State University, 107
Chingos, 94

Clanchy, 62

Clark, 119

Coalition on the Academic Workforce, 8, 16

Cohen, 50

collaboration, learning, 39-40

Coley, C., 95, 96, 97, 99 . .

Coley, T., 95, 96, 97, 99

Collins, 53, 54

Community-Campus Partnerships for Health (CCPH), 113

community involvement, 103-115
    contemporary, 104-107
    drawbacks, 113-114
    historical, 103-104
    technology, 112-113

Concordia University, 8, 16

contingent faculty, *See* non-tenure track

Coopman, 131

Coursera, 133

Cragg, 49, 50

Cranton, 68

critical compassionate pedagogy, 37

critical thinking, 62

Cuban, 108

Currie, 63

Curry, J., 75, 76, 79, 81, 82

Curry, T.H., 15, 17

Curwood, 113, 114

Cuseo, 91, 93, 100

Cushner, 111

D

Daggett, 103, 108

Dahme, 63

Dakota State University (DSU), 17, 18, 19, 20, 21

Davenport, 31, 38

Davis, 27, 32, 42

Dean, 39

Dede, 118, 119, 120, 121, 124

Delen, 91, 92

DiGeronimo, 30

Digital Media Simulation, 112

Doyle, 32

Dreon, 136

Duke University, 133

E

EDUCAUSE, 134

Eaton, 29

Elder, 62

Englander, 20

Engle, 11, 27

Ehrenberg, 123

Estrella, 40

evaluation, *See also* professoriate
    teaching, 17-18
    scholarship, 19-20
    service, 20-21

F

Facebook, 134, 135, 136

Faculty Focus, 136

faculty role
    student retention, 27-45
    See scholarly writing

Fahnoe, 107

Farrar, 113, 114

Filkins, 32

Filipczak, 51

first-generation students, *See* retention

Friedman, 104

Friedrich, 61

Frolich, 91

G

Gaines 7, 8, 61

Gardner, 33

Gelmon, 113

Gengel, B., 110

Gengel, C., 110

Gengel, G., 110

Gilbert, 104

Goldberger, 62, 66
Goodwin College, 111
Google, 104
Google Hangouts, 134, 136
Gordon, 96
Gregg, 38
Groom, 134
groups, 49-59
Gross, 106
Grow Your Own Teachers, 107, 108
Groysberg, 78, 79, 80

H

Habley, 96
Hackman, 8, 16
Hagenauer, 58
Hainline 7, 8, 61
Hall, 16, 23
Hanover Research, 136
Hao, 37
    critical compassionate pedagogy, 37
Hargreaves, 49
Harper, 29, 38, 39, 40, 42, 43, 44
Harris, 62, 65
Harvard University, 91, 133
Harvey, 39, 44
Hattie, 65, 66
Heaps, 61
Hewlett Foundation, 134
Higgins, 69, 70
Hill, 75, 77, 80, 81, 84, 127, 129
hiring, See professoriate
Hoover, 90
Housel, 39, 44
Howe, 121, 122, 123
Hughes, 49
Humphreys, 50
Hurt, 56, 57
Hussar, 91
Hyland, 63, 64, 66
Hyon, 63

I

IDEO, 104
Industrial Revolution, 117
Information Age, 117
Institute for Higher Education Policy
    (IHEP), 27, 28, 38, 43
iTunes, 133

J

Jalomo, 38
Jean, 134
Jehangir, 29, 30
Jensen, 56, 108
Johns, 64, 65
Jordan, C., 113
Jordan, T., 7, 118, 120, 121, 122, 123

K

Kennedy, 109
Kena, 91
Kadison, 30
Kelley, 107
Kemp, 91
Kereluik, 107
Kezar, 8, 16
Khan, 134
Khan Academy, 14, 134
Kinzie, 94, 95, 96, 99
Kisker, 50
Kononova, 63
Krull, 30
Kuh, 96, 99

L

Laist, 109, 112
Lamott, 68
Latham, 106, 107
Lattuca, 51
Lawless, 39
Learning Partnerhips Model, 39

learning styles, 38-39, 40, 51-52
Lehman, 88, 89, 90
Leki, 63, 64, 70
Lemmer, 118, 119, 124
Leonard, 110, 111
Levessaur, 64
Lindsey, 117
Literacies Framework, 105
Long Feather 7, 8, 61
Lorenzetti, 99
Lotkowski, 87
low-income students, *See* retention
Lucas, 111, 133
Lupi, 110, 111
Lynch-Holmes, 95, 96, 97, 99

M

Ma, 119
Mackeigan, 113, 114
MacPherson, 94
Mader, 12, 62
Magna Publications, 95
Mahon, 111
Mandelbaum, 104
Marcia, 40
Marques, 133
Martinez, J.A., 30
Martinez, M., 50
Massachusetts Institute of Technology (MIT), 133, 134
Massive Open Online Courses (MOOCs), 13, 132, 133, 134, 139
McCarthy, 8, 16
McDaniel, 67
McEntee, 51, 58
McFarlane, 109
McGinley, 113
McGuire, 133
McKay, 40
McKee, 77, 82, 83, 84
Merriam-Webster, 135

Meshing College, 104
Michael, 28, 29, 134
Middlebury College, 17, 18, 19, 20, 22
Millar, 38
Milligan, 135
Mishra, 107
Mitchell, 113, 114
Moodle (Modular Object Oriented Dynamic Learning Environment), 130, 131, 132, 135, 138
Moodle Basics for Instructors, 132
Munger, 113, 114
Murray, 120, 122

N

Nairn, 69, 70
National Council of Teachers of English (NCTE), 105, 106
National Education Association (NEA), 22
National Online Learners' Priorities Report, 128
National Survey of Student Engagement (NSSE), 94
Newton's First Law of Motion, 96
Nilson, 68
Noel-Levitz, 128, 129
Noeth, 87
non-tenure-track, 8
non-traditional-age students, 53
Northern Illinois University, 131

O

Olin College, 104
OnlineCollege.org, 135
Open Educational Resources (OERs), 14, 132, 134, 139
OpenCourseWare, 134
OpenYaleCourse (Yale Center for Teaching and Learning), 133
Oregon, 131
Oregon State University (OSU), 18, 19
Orwell, 65

Ostrander, 114

P

PC Magazine, 135
Padilla 7, 8, 61
Paul, 62
Pelletier, 130, 136
Pew Research Center, 61
Piercy, 67
Pink, 106
Plater, 16, 23
Points of Light, 109
Pollack, 89
Prior, 65
professoriate
    changing expectations, 9-11
    community involvement, 103-115
    evaluation, 16-22 *See also* evaluation
    hiring, 15-16 *See also* hiring
    identity, 117-125
    keys to success,123-124
    leadership, 75-85
    leadership skills, 77-80
    promotion, 16 *See also* promotion
    See also retention, student
    See also virtual teaching
promotion, *See also* professoriate
    process, 21-22
    tenure, 22
Purcell, 61, 70

Q

Quaye, 29, 38, 39, 40, 42, 43, 44

R

recruitment, student, 87-100
    faculty involvement, 90-91
    institutional role, 91-92
    team, 89-90
Reeves, 78, 83
Renden, 38
retention, student, 27-45, 87-100
    academic advising, 42-43
    faculty engagement, 88

    faculty influence, 92-93
    faculty role, 31-32
    faculty strategies, 93-95
    first-generation, 27-31, 39, 40, 41
    institutional role, 43-44
    low income, 27-31, 39
    mentoring, 95-
    role of relationships, 27-44
Rice, 118
Richardson, 65
Robins, 87
Ronald, 65
Roney, 15

S

SCAMPER, 54
STEM, 43
SWOT, 54
Saddler, 67
Sadler, 66
Saltzman, 21, 22
SCAMPER, 54
Schloss, 49, 50
Schuh, 96, 99
Schuster, 117, 118
scholarly writing, 61-71
    critical thinking, 62
    discourse, 63-65
    emotions, 69-70
    feedback, 65-67, 68
    rubrics, 67
Sedlacek, 51, 52
Seifer, 113
service learning, 40-41
Sheehy, 61
Sher, 30
Shwom, 55
Siegel, 31, 38
Skinner, 107, 108
Smith, B.,50
Smith, C., 87, 88
Smith College, 132
Snyder, 55

Soria, 95, 98, 99

Sprenkle, 67

Stamats Communications, 88

Stanford, 133

Stark, 51

State University of New York, 112

Steele, 98

Straumsheim, 132

Strauss, 121, 122, 123

Strohl, 87

Stuber, 30

SWOT, 54

Syracuse University, 96

Szbinski 7, 118, 120, 121, 122, 123

T

TED Conferences, 136

TED Talks, 14, 134, 135, 136, 138

Tahan, 91

Taub, 95

Teaching Center at Washington University, 68

tenure
    track, 8
    promotion, 22

Terenzini, 38

Terrell, 28

Terry, E., 7, 8, 61

Terry, L., 107

Thill, 55

Timperley, 66

Tinto, 11, 27, 28, 31, 91, 92, 93, 94, 96, 97, 98, 99

Tolchinsky, 63

Toolwire, 112

Toor, 65

Tresey, 118, 119, 120, 121

Trembley, 88, 89, 90

Twitter, 134, 135, 136

Tyack, 108

U

Udacity, 133

Udemy, 133

Ulerick, 15

Umbach, 41

University of Auckland, 65

University of California, Los Angeles (UCLA), 105, 133

University of California, Berkeley, 133

University of Cincinnati, 131

University of Colorado, 22

University of Washington, 17, 18, 19, 20, 22

Upcraft, 33, 38, 40, 41

Uzuner-Smith, 20

V

Venable, 135

Villegas, 111

virtual teaching, 127-138
    delivery, 129-130
    learners, 128-129
    online resources, 132-134
    principles of, 136-138
    social media, 134-136
    platforms, 130-132

Volet, 58

W

Wagner, 104

Walker, 95

Ward, 31, 38

Watkins, 107, 112

Watson, L.W., 28,

Watson, J., 129, 130

Wawrzynski, 41

Whitt, 96, 99

Wikis, 55

Wilfrid Laurier University, 113

Wilkins, 28, 29

Williams, 57

Willis, 53, 54, 56, 57
Witte, 106
Wolfe, 49, 51, 52, 54, 56
Wolff, 49
work experience, student, *See* ABT
Wood, 30
World Wide Web, 129
Wright, 28

Wulff, 117

Y

Yale University, 133
You Tube, 133, 134, 135, 136, 138
Young, 51, 52, 127, 134

Z

Zepeda, 51

About the Primary Authors

Nicholas D. Young, PhD, EdD

Dr. Nicholas D. Young has worked in diverse educational roles for more than 28 years, serving as a principal, special education director, graduate professor, graduate program director, graduate dean, and longtime superintendent of schools. He was named the Massachusetts Superintendent of the Year, and completed a distinguished Fulbright program focused on the Japanese educational system through the collegiate level. Dr. Young is the recipient of numerous other honors and recognitions including the General Douglas MacArthur Award for distinguished civilian and military leadership and the Vice Admiral John T. Hayward Award for exemplary scholarship. He holds several graduate degrees including a PhD in educational administration and an EdD in educational psychology.

Dr. Young has served in the U.S. Army and U.S. Army Reserves combined for over 33 years; he graduated with distinction from the U.S. Air War College, the U.S. Army War College, and the U.S. Navy War College. After completing a series of senior leadership assignments in the U.S. Army Reserves as the commanding officer of the 287th Medical Company (DS), the 405th Area Support Company (DS), the 405th Combat Support Hospital, and 399 Combat Support Hospital, he transitioned to his current military position as a faculty instructor at the U.S. Army War College in Carlisle, Pennsylvania. He holds the rank of Colonel.

Dr. Young is also a regular presenter at state, national, and international conferences, and he has written many books, book chapters, and articles on various topics in education, counseling, and psychology. Some of his most recent books include *From Lecture Hall to Laptop: Opportunities, Challenges, and the Continuing Evolution of Virtual Learning in Higher Education* (in press) and *Learning Style Perspectives: Impact upon the Classroom* (3rd ed. 2014) and *Collapsing Educational Boundaries from Preschool to PhD: Building Bridges Across the Educational Spectrum* (2013). He was also a primary author for *To Campus with Confidence: Promoting a Smooth Transition to College for Stu-*

dents with Learning Disabilities (in-press), *Educational Entrepreneurship: Promoting Public-Private Partnerships for the 21st Century* (2015), *Beyond the Bedtime Story: Promoting Reading Development During the Middle School Years* (2015), *Betwixt and Between: Understanding and Meeting the Social and Emotional Developmental Needs of Students During the Middle School Transition Years* (2014), *Transforming Special Education Practices: A Primer for School Administrators and Policy Makers* (2012) and *Powerful Partners in Student Success: Schools, Families and Communities* (2012). He has also coauthored several children's books to include the popular series, I Am Full of Possibilities. Dr. Young may be contacted at nyoung1191@aol.com.

Lynne M. Celli, PhD

Dr. Lynne M. Celli has devoted her career to education at all levels for more than 35 years. She has been a teacher, principal, superintendent of schools, professor, and chair of a graduate program. Currently, Dr. Celli is the associate dean of graduate education programs at Endicott College in Beverly, Massachusetts. She earned her PhD and MEd in curriculum, instruction, and administration from Boston College and her BA in sociology/education from Clark University. Her primary research interests are focused on leadership in higher education as well as the connections between high-quality teaching strategies and student learning styles. Dr. Celli has authored and co-authored several books, book chapters and articles, Some of her most recent work includes co-authoring *Learning Style Perspectives: Impact Upon the Classroom* (3rd edtion 2014) and *Collapsing Educational Boundaries from Preschool to PhD: Building Bridges Across the Educational Spectrum* (2013). She presents regularly at international and national conferences. Dr. Celli may be contacted at cellilynne@aol.com.

About the Chapter Authors

Nadine Bonda, PhD

Dr. Nadine Bonda has worked in education for over 40 years, holding positions of superintendent, assistant superintendent, principal, mathematics department chair, and mathematics teacher. She was headmaster of a school for students with dyslexia and language processing problems. In addition, Dr. Bonda has taught leadership and mathematics pedagogy at the University of British Columbia. Presently, she is an assistant professor at American International College, teaching qualitative research in the doctoral programs in educational leadership as well as teaching and learning. Dr. Bonda also works as a consultant, primarily on projects involving the improvement of underperforming schools and districts and matters concerning school and district accountability. She holds a PhD in curriculum and instruction from the University of British Columbia, a CAGS in leadership from Boston University, an MEd in mathematics from Boston University, and a BA in mathematics from Regis College. She has written many articles, and her writing has appeared in several books.

Dr. Bonda may be contacted at nbonda@comcast.net.

Linda E. Denault, EdD

Dr. Linda Denault is a professor in the education department at Becker College and an assistant professor in the low-residency doctoral program at American International College. Prior to joining the faculty in higher education, she held numerous positions in K–12 public education, serving as a classroom teacher, assistant principal, principal, curriculum coordinator, and superintendent of schools. In addition, Dr. Denault has presented at conferences regionally, nationally, and internationally, and she has authored chapters of several education-related books. She holds a BS, MEd, and CAGS from Worcester State and earned her doctorate in educational research, policy, and administration from the University of Massachusetts–Amherst.

Dr. Denault may be contacted at ledenault@aol.com.

Janice A. Fedor, EdD, MBA

Dr. Janice A. Fedor holds a bachelor's degree and an MBA from the University of Massachusetts–Amherst and a doctorate in educational leadership and supervision from American International College. She has taught various college courses since 2004, including management, marketing, organizational behavior, marketing research, sales and selling, and gender and diversity management. She has been involved with Junior Achievement at the secondary and postsecondary levels and has been a faculty advisor for student case competition teams. Dr. Fedor is active with the International Accreditation of Collegiate Business Educators (IACBE) organization and mentors student teams who compete in regional and national competitions. Her most recent work was *Cohort Models of Learning: Adapting Content to Women's Learning Styles* (ProQuest 2016). Dr. Fedor may be contacted at janicefedor1@comcast.net.

Elizabeth Jean, EdD

Dr. Elizabeth Jean has served as an elementary school educator and administrator in various rural and urban settings in Massachusetts for more than 20 years. As a building administrator, she has been instrumental in fostering partnerships with local businesses and higher education institutions. Further, she is currently a graduate adjunct professor at Endicott College and previously taught at Our Lady of the Elms College. Dr. Jean received a BS in education from Springfield College, an MEd in education with a concentration in reading from Our Lady of the Elms, and an EdD in curriculum, teaching, learning, and leadership from Northeastern University. Dr. Jean has coauthored *From Lecture Hall to Laptop: Opportunities, Challenges, and the Continuing Evolution of Virtual Learning in Higher Education* (in press). She has also written book chapters on such topics as virtual education, public and private partnerships in public education, technology partnerships between K-12 and higher education, developing a stategic mindset for LD students, the importance of skill and will in developing reading habits for young children, and middle school reading interventions. She also has coauthored and illustrated several children's books. Dr. Jean may be contacted at elizabethjean1221@gmail.com.

Judith L. Klimkiewicz, EdD

Dr. Judith L. Klimkiewicz is a recently retired superintendent of schools for the Nashoba Valley Technical School District, a position she held for over 20 years. She previously served as the Commonwealth of Massachusetts' state director of career and technical education for several years, during a time when significant statewide and national education reforms were implemented. Dr. Klimkiewicz recently returned to the Massachusetts Department of Education to serve as a senior consultant for strategic planning for college/career education and workforce development. In this current role, she advises the Commissioner, the Board of Education, and the Executive Office of the Governor on key issues related to college and career training. Dr. Klimkiewicz may be reached at gklimkiewicz@rcn.com.

Christine N. Michael, PhD

Dr. Christine N. Michael is a 40-year educational veteran with a variety of professional experiences. She holds degrees from Brown University, Rhode Island College, Union Institute and University, and the University of Connecticut, where she earned a PhD in education, human development, and family relations. Her previous work has included middle and high school teaching, higher education administration, college teaching, and educational consulting. She has also been involved with Head Start, Upward Bound, national nonprofit Foundation for Excellent Schools and College for Every Student, and the federal Trio programs. She has published widely on topics in education and psychology, most recently as a primary author and coeditor for the book *Betwixt and Between: Understanding and Meeting the Social and Emotional Development Needs of Students During the Middle School Transition Years* (2014) and *Beyond the Bedtime Story: Promoting Reading Development During the Middle School Years* (2015). She is currently the program director of low-residency programs at American International College. Dr. Michael may be contacted at cnevadam@gmail.com.

Rick Roque, EdD

Dr. Rick Roque is the author of dozens of articles on U.S. banking and finance topics and is a thoughtful leader in education finance and educational leadership in the United States and developing countries. He works and has an active interest in K–12 and higher education in emerging markets. His consulting work has centered on capital fundraising, researching state and local funding formulas, establishing public-private partnerships, and resource/expansion planning. Dr. Roque has spoken at conferences in Europe and worked in Africa and the Middle East with higher education institutions on local growth opportunities. He completed his EdD at American International College while conducting research in establishing alternative revenue models for K–12 and higher education in the US. Dr. Roque may be contacted at rick@menlocompany.com.